How to Stay Alive and Well in the Fast Lane!

MW00512093

A Survival Kit
by

Pamela Smith, Registered Dietitian

and

Carolyn Coats

Illustrations by Sheila Behr

Thomas Nelson Publishers - Nashville

Table of Contents

Foreword   2
Introduction   4
Ten Commandments of Good Nutrition   7
Commandment I Breakfast Breaks the Fast   9
Commandment II Snacks are Smart   13
Power Snack List   17
Seven Health Habits for a Longer Life   19
Commandment III The Protein and Carbo Balance   20
The Ten Best and Worst Foods   30
Commandment IV Double That Fiber!   32
Commandment V Trim That Fat!   39
Ten Terrific Reasons to Exercise   47
Rating the Fats   50
Super Substitutes   54
Commandment VI Eat Your Fruits and Veggies   58

Commandment VII Vitamins-Food Not Pills 62
Commandment VIII Water, That Magic Potion 67
Commandment IX Salt, Sugar, Caffeine, Alcohol 71
Healthy Hints for Good Nutrition 85
Super Quick Weight Loss Diet 88
Commandment X Fad Diet Facts 89
"Have It Your Way" Weight Loss Plan for Women 92
Maintenance Plan for Women 94
"Have It Your Way" Weight Loss Plan for Men 94
Maintenance Plan for Men 96
Your Grocery List for Health 98
A Guide to Eating Out All Over America 101
Perfect Breakfast Menus with Recipes 115
Easy Lunches with Recipes 121
Delicious Dinner Menus with Recipes 125
Quick Meals for the Fast Laners 140
Holiday and Party Entertaining 143

Dear friends,

As many of you know, I wrote my first book, "Things Your Mother Always Told You But You Didn't Want To Hear" when my children were leaving the nest. My life changed dramatically as I moved from being a homemaker to a book publisher as the book became a bestseller. As I began to do an enormous amount of traveling, I discovered a whole new set of problems. Constant eating out, a schedule that made normal meal timing impossible and huge demands on my energy level soon made me eat more, hoping to get more energy. Unfortunately, eating more did not give me more energy, only more weight.

I finally got desperate. I made an appointment with Pam Smith, the nutritionist who was working miracles with so many in Florida. Her patients were reaching their ideal weight, had higher energy levels and looked healthier after going to her.

Pam had the specific knowledge for putting my good intentions to work. Unlike the many diets I had been on in the past, she put more emphasis on _what_ I should be eating, _when_ I should be eating and _why_ I should be eating it. She stressed balance and moderation, nothing radical. The main thing she did was educate me.

She encouraged me to adopt an exercise program to increase my metabolism as well as my total fitness. I chose walking because I can do it any time or any place.

Following Pams' "Have It Your Way" meal plan (which we have included for you) I began to shed my excess weight and so did my husband. Best of all, I found that eating for wellness gave me back the high energy level I had as a youth.

I highly recommend that you Eat Well to Live Well.

Sincerely,
Carolyn Coate

3

Alive and Well in the Fast Lane

We hope you enjoy this book. We've tried to make it a book that would teach you everything you ever wanted to know about nutrition and, in addition, give you a unique, effective nutritional meal plan that lets _you_ make the choices. You will be able to enjoy your favorite restaurant or dine anywhere around the world because you will know how to make the _right_ choices! You will also learn what to eat, when to eat and how much to eat for peak stamina and performance. It really is a "Have it Your Way" plan in which you are in control of your body, your energy level, your maximum healing ability and your own well-being. It is a formula for good health and lean bodies.

The "Dining Out Guide" will be helpful to you in making good choices in the fanciest restaurants and the fastest food places, your favorite deli, anywhere!

Our <u>Ten Commandments</u> are guidelines for a longer, healthier life and the "<u>Ten Best and Ten Worst</u> food list will provide you with the way to know the beautiful foods that make beautiful bodies.

The <u>Power Snacks</u> list will let you maintain a high energy level and keep you from overeating at the next meal. People will be amazed to watch you eat fruits, cheeses, bread, crackers, pasta and trail-mix; all foods the dieting world has feared. You will not be deprived or hungry with this plan!

For parties and holidays, we've suggested menus that take your favorite recipes, reduce the fat, increase the fiber and make them into healthy old friends. These "<u>Tips for Holiday Health</u>" show you how to survive, yet have a great time, by focusing attention on celebrating the joy of being with family and friends, not on overeating.

The list of <u>Super Substitutes</u> will enable you to keep many of the things you love in your diet by

5

changing them to make them tasty but still healthy. Thus it will help you attain your ideal fat to muscle ratio quickly.

We've even included a section on "Preparing Quick Meals," those that take less time to prepare than to eat.

To top off this entire lifestyle package, we've included wonderful "Breakfasts, Lunches and Dinners" that you can use as a blueprint for a terrific way of cooking and eating. These recipes are simple to prepare and the meals are perfectly balanced in carbohydrates and protein. They also contain a wealth of variety to keep you out of a boring rut because having a different breakfast, lunch and dinner everyday makes life a lot more exciting.

The "7 Health Habits to Help You Live Longer" will speed you on your way to total health.

Enjoy your new wellness!

The 10 Commandments of Nutrition

I Thou shalt never skip breakfast.

II Thou shalt eat every 3 to 4 hours and have your healthy snack handy.

III Thou shalt always eat a carbohydrate with a protein.

IV Thou shalt double your fiber.

V Thou shalt trim the fat from your diet.

VI Thou shalt believe your mother was right: Eat your fruits and veggies.

VII Thou shalt get your vitamins from food not pills.

VIII Thou shalt drink at least 8 glasses of water a day.

IX Thou shalt use a minimum of salt, sugar, caffeine and alcohol.

X Thou shalt never go on a fad diet.

Ist Commandment:
Thou shalt never skip breakfast.

1st Commandment: Thou shalt never skip breakfast.

If you want to start your day with a boundless energy level, your metabolism in high gear and proteins actively healing and building new cells, then "Thou shalt never skip breakfast!"

Think of your body as a campfire that dies down during the night and in the morning needs to be stoked up with wood to begin to burn vigorously again. Without stoking, the fire will die down with no flame or sparks. Your body is very similar; it awakens in a slowed, fasting state. You must "break the fast" with breakfast to rev up the body into high gear. If you choose not to eat breakfast, the body not only stays slowed down, but as in the case of the campfire, the metabolism will die down even more. Starving your body all day will keep it dragging through the day in a slowed down metabolic state and when the evening gorge begins, most of that food will have to be stored as fat. All that food can't possibly be burned up because the body isn't burning energy at a fast rate because the fire has gone out. The food that comes in is like dumping an armload of firewood on a dead fire! Don't think for a minute that you are saving calories by skipping breakfast or your healthy snacks; those calories would have been burned by the higher metabolic rate. You are only starving your body of valuable carbohydrates that burn to give you energy and proteins that build the new you.

I bet you've said this, 'If I skip breakfast, I don't get hungry till later in the day but if I eat breakfast I get hungry every few hours. You're right! This means your body is working correctly. When you starve your body in the morning, waste products are released into your system that temporarily depress your appetite and allow you to continue to starve without feeling hungry for many hours. Unfortunately you are 1- letting your body go into a low metabolic gear and 2. setting yourself up for a gorge and as soon as you begin to eat, your appetite is "really" turned on! Not only will you overeat because your blood sugar has fallen so low, but, like the campfire, your body will not be able to burn those calories well. Remember, your body just cannot use such a large intake of food at one time, it will be stored as fat and the nutrients will be wasted.

<u>Healthy goal</u>: Start your day with a boundless energy level, your metabolism in high gear and proteins actively healing and building new cells and NEVER SKIP BREAKFAST!

Don't think you are necessarily on the right track just because it's a well-beaten path.

2nd Commandment: Thou shalt eat every 3 to 4 hours and have your healthy snack handy.

13

2nd Commandment: Thou shalt eat every 3 to 4 hours and have your healthy snack handy.

Smaller, more frequent meals will result in more energy, better weight loss, and easier weight maintenance. Several small meals a day deposit less fat than one or two large meals, even if you eat the same food and the same amount.

Remember the campfire story. Healthy snacking is very much like throwing wood on a fire all through the day to keep it burning well. Your body was created to survive and it reads long hours without food as starvation, dramatically slowing down rather than burn your valuable muscle mass. Contrary to what you think, in a starvation state when no carbohydrate is available, your body turns first to muscle mass for energy and to your fat stores last. You must keep your body fed the right thing at the right time for it to metabolize calories efficiently, burning them for energy rather than your muscle.

Establish consistent eating patterns including 3 meals a day with at least one snack. Ideally, you should eat 25% of your calories at breakfast, 25% at lunch, 25% at dinner and the other 25% as healthy snacks through the day.

<u>Healthy Goal:</u> If you want to take in food in the healthiest and most usuable way, Thou Shalt Eat Every 3 to 4 Hours and Have your Healthy Snack Handy. Taking in small amounts of food 5 to 6 times a day, keeps the body from storing excess calories as fat and keeps your blood sugar and energy level up and even, so you have maximum stamina all through the day.

Nothing tastes as good as being healthy feels.

The more you prepare, the luckier you get.

Always, Always have your healthy snack handy.

When most people think of snacks, they think of potato chips, candy bars and sodas. This type of snack can be nutritionally and calorically disastrous! They provide high amounts of fat, sugar and salt and little or no nutritional value. But you _can_ enjoy healthy snacks that will prevent your blood sugar from dropping too low leaving you sleepy and craving sweets. They will keep your metabolism burning high, your stomach feeling full and satisfied, and still not load you with unwanted, unneeded fat and sugar.

<u>Healthy Goal:</u> Have your snack handy - at home, in your car, in your desk drawer. You _must_ plan ahead! When you go too long without food, you're likely to grab an unhealthy snack if you're not prepared.

Power Snack Ideas

♥ Whole grain crackers and lowfat cheese
♥ Fresh fruit and lowfat cheese
♥ Plain yogurt blended with unsweetened fruit. Try crushed pineapple, applesauce or the new "All Fruit Preserves."
♥ Whole grain cereal with skim milk
♥ Popcorn sprinkled with parmesan cheese
♥ Pita bread with lowfat cheese, heated together. Add some tomato sauce for a pita pizza.
♥ Whole wheat English muffin with non-fat cream cheese and "All Fruit Preserves"
♥ No oil tortilla chips with fat-free bean dip
♥ ½ sandwich (great to freeze and take along to thaw.)
♥ Oat bran or whole wheat muffin and skim milk
♥ Small pop-top can of tuna or chicken packed in water and crackers
♥ Rice cakes and lowfat cheese
♥ Wasa bread, dijon mustard and sliced turkey

17

♥Trail Mix - The easiest and favorite one.
    1 cup dry roasted, unsalted peanuts
    1 cup dry roasted or raw sunflower seeds
    2 cups raisins - dark or light
Make in abundance and bag up in ¼ cup batches
  for women and ½ cup for men. <u>In these
    portions</u>, this balanced snack gives you
    all the good fiber and protein of peanuts
    but not too much of its fat and calories.

The 7 Health Habits to Help You Live Longer

1. Buckle up-every time
2. Eat 3 meals a day plus healthy snacks.
3. Eat moderately. Don't overeat or undereat.
4. No cigarette smoking at all.
5. Exercise regularly-at least 20 minutes, 3 times a week.
6. Moderate to no use of alcohol
7. Get 7 to 8 hours of sleep a night.

Good health has more to do with everyday behavior and habits than with miracles of medical science.

Prevention of disease is far superior to cure!

3rd Commandment: Thou shalt always
have a carbohydrate with a protein.

3rd Commandment. Thou shalt always eat a protein with a carbohydrate.

Carbohydrate is 100% pure energy. It should be eaten with protein to protect protein from being wasted as a less efficient source of energy. This allows protein to be used for its vital functions: boosting your metabolism, building body muscle, Keeping body fluids in balance, healing and fighting infection and making beautiful skin, hair and nails. Always remember, Carbohydrates burn and proteins build!

What is a carbohydrate?

1. Anything that comes from a plant is a carbohydrate (pg. 23). Plants convert sunlight into carbohydrate, our bodies convert carbohydrate to energy.
2. Carbohydrates are the only source of fiber.
3. Carbohydrates are 100% pure energy.
4. Carbohydrates are low calorie, contrary to all you've heard! 1 ounce of carbos is ½ the calories

of 1 ounce of fat. It's not the bread and potatoes that make you fat, it's the butter, toppings and sauces we put on them. Don't throw them out, just modify what you put on them. See page 54 for super substitutes.

5. Carbohydrates burn and proteins build. Never believe anybody or anything that tells you not to eat carbohydrate or not to eat it with protein. You will be robbing your body of energy all day long.

Don't be afraid to ask dumb questions They're easier to handle than dumb mistakes.

Discipline is doing what doesn't come naturally.

Where are carbohydrates found?

Complex carbohydrates are found in:

1 - The grains - Bread, crackers, pasta, cereal, rice, wild rice, oatmeal, barley and grits.
2 - The starchy vegetables - Potatoes, white and sweet, peas, winter squash, turnips, black-eyed peas, lima beans, corn and parsnips.

Simple carbohydrates are found in:

1 - Fruits and fruit juices
2 - Non-starchy vegetables - any vegetable other than the starchy vegetables listed above.
3 - Sugars

Leaders are ordinary people with extraordinary determination.

23

What Is A Protein?

1- Anything that comes from an animal gives you complete protein. A complete protein is one that supplies all the essential amino acids, those the body can't make and doesn't store. Legumes, although a plant food and incomplete in essential amino acids, are also excellent proteins.

2- Protein is the new you! Protein makes muscles that shape your body, it makes new hair, new nails and beautifies your skin. It works to replace worn out cells and to regulate your body's functions. Protein is so important that you cannot be healthy, not even attractive, without it. Protein is so powerful that we don't need very much of it; as a matter of fact, a 6 ½ oz. can of chicken provides all the protein you need for the whole day. "A little dab will do you" certainly applies to protein. The typical American diet provides us with 2 to 3 times the amount recommended. The amount of protein eaten is not the only secret to a healthy, beautiful body; protein is <u>not</u> stored, so it must be replenished frequently throughout the day, each and every day of your life! The protein and carbohydrate you eat is the fuel on which your body runs.

Misconceptions about Protein

Never, never believe anybody or anything that tells you that you don't need protein, or to eat it only once a day. You are robbing your body of proteins healing and building power all day long.

The diets of our time have promised it to be the food to eat for weight loss, and the truth is that an all-protein, no carbohydrate diet so imbalances the body that you do lose weight but all water and muscle, and little or no fat. A balanced intake of protein <u>with</u> carbohydrate is essential to lose the right kind of weight while keeping your health.

25

Where are proteins found?

Complete protein is found in dairy products, eggs, fish, seafood, poultry, beef, pork and lamb.

One of the drawbacks of the American problem of overeating protein is that most of the popular protein foods are high in fat and fat is the major dietary risk factor in the killer diseases. By choosing the lower fat versions of protein foods you will get all of their goodness (protein, calcium, magnesium, iron and zinc) without the risk.

Ideal low fat protein sources

♥ Lowfat cheeses: Farmer's cheese, Mozzarella (part-skim) Weight Watcher's Natural cheddar, Kraft Natural Light, any part-skim milk cheese (1 oz. gives 1 oz. protein.)

♥ 1% or 2% lowfat cottage cheese. 1/4 cup = 1 oz. protein

♥ Part-skimmed Ricotta - 1/4 cup = 1 oz. protein

♥ Non-fat or Low-fat Yogurt. 1/2 cup = 1 oz. protein

♥ Lowfat and skimmed milk - Skimmed milk is the only complete protein without fat.- 1/2 cup = 1 oz. protein

More Low Fat Protein Sources

♥ Eggs - 1 egg = 1 oz. protein
♥ Fish - 1 oz. = 1 oz. protein - ¼ cup water packed tuna, salmon = 1 oz. protein.
♥ Seafood - 5 shrimp, oysters, scallops or clams equals 1 oz. protein; ¼ cup crab or lobster = 1 oz.
♥ Chicken - 1 oz. = 1 oz. protein. 1 small split breast = 2 oz. protein, 1 large split breast = 3 oz. protein. 1 leg = 1 oz. protein, 1 leg, thigh combo = 3 oz. protein and 1 small whole breast equals about 4 oz. protein.
♥ Turkey - 1 oz. = 1 oz. protein
♥ Veal - 1 oz. = 1 oz. protein
♥ Lean beef - 1 oz. = 1 oz. protein. Beef generally loses 25% of its weight in cooking.
♥ Lean, well-trimmed pork 1 oz. = 1 oz. protein
♥ Lean lamb - 1 oz. = 1 oz. protein

Some people think the three basic food groups are canned, frozen and take-out.

Where are incomplete proteins found?

Legumes: Soybeans, Pinto beans, Split peas, Lentils Kidney Beans, Black Beans, Red Beans, Navy Beans, Peanuts, Natural Peanut Butter

Legumes, although a plant food, contain enough valuable protein to be considered an excellent source of high-fiber, low-fat protein. They are considered "incomplete" proteins because they each lack sufficient amounts of one or more of the essential amino acids. They <u>must</u> be eaten with a grain (corn, wheat, rice oats) or a seed (sunflower, sesame) to be complete. Examples: peanut butter on bread, black beans over rice, beans and cornbread or tortillas, peanut and sunflower seed mix. Generally, 1/2 cup of cooked beans serves as 2 oz. of protein when mixed with an appropriate grain or seed and 3/4 cup will equal 3 oz. protein.

<u>Your Healthy Goal:</u> Smaller amounts of protein balanced with carbohydrates eaten in evenly distributed amounts through the day.

Beautiful Foods for Beautiful Bodies

There are certain foods that carry a powerful punch. They're loaded with the vitamins and minerals your body needs to look and feel its very best. Get more of these into your diet and you'll see a big difference in your hair, skin, nails, energy level and well-being right away. Looking and feeling good is an inside-out job.

<u>Healthy Goal:</u> Learn the 10 Best and 10 Worst Foods and increase the best and eliminate the worst and see how much better you feel— and look!

29

Ten Best Foods

1. Broccoli
2. Chicken or turkey
3. Fish-especially cold water fish because of their valuable EPA oil.
4. Legumes (dried beans and peanuts)
5. Oranges
6. Potatoes (white and sweet)
7. Skim or low-fat dairy products
8. Spinach
9. Strawberries
10. Whole grains (breads, cereals, crackers, rice and pasta)

Ten Worst Foods (~~FOODS~~)

1. Artificial fruit drinks - nothing more than sugar, water with artificial flavor and coloring added.

2. Bacon, corned beef, ham, pastrami, salami and sausage Loaded with saturated fats, salt and preservatives

3. Breakfast or granola bars - candy bars rolled in oats! Loaded with sugar and fat.

4. Chocolate - high in saturated fat, caffeine and sugar.

5. Donuts - white flour and sugar fried in animal fat.

6. Hot dogs, bologna and all processed meats - high in saturated fat, salt and preservatives that have been linked to cancer.

7. Liver - high in iron as it may be, it is an animal's filter that collects the insecticides, poisons and cholesterol.

8. Snack chips and french fries - Triple threats: high in saturated fats, salt and calories.

9. Sodas - most have 12 teaspoons sugar per can along with artificial flavoring, coloring and most have caffeine. Diet sodas contain all the above only use chemical sweetener along with the sodium.

10. Sugar

4th Commandment: Thou shalt double your fiber.

32

4th Commandment: Thou shalt double your fiber.

Grandma used to say "Eat your roughage" and now, years later, the Surgeon General says, "Double your fiber." This can be done rather easily; not with fiber pills but by increasing your intake of whole grain breads and cereals, unprocessed bran, beans, fresh fruits and vegetables.

What is Fiber?

1. Fiber is the part of plants not digested by the body.
2. There are two types of fiber: The <u>soluble fibers</u> and the <u>non-soluble fibers</u>. The <u>soluble</u> fibers are found in apples, dried beans, peanuts, barley and America's new miracle food, oatmeal and oat bran. These soluble fibers have been found to lower cholesterol and triglycerides and to help control blood sugar levels. This works by the fiber capturing the cholesterol in the intestines, taking the cholesterol out of the body. 33

The <u>Non-soluble fibers</u> are found in wheat bran, whole grain breads, cereals, fruits and vegetables. They are excellent means of controlling constipation, diverticulosis, diarrhea and possibly preventing hemorrhoids.

3- Think of fiber as a sponge which absorbs excess water in the G.I track to curtail diarrhea but provides a bulky mass which will move through more easily and quickly to relieve constipation and diverticulosis.

You need <u>both</u> soluble and non soluble and <u>lots</u> of wonderful water to keep the body working at its best! The soluble fiber adds bulk and softness to the stool and the non-soluble moves it along, but fiber needs water to make it work the way it should; ideally 8 to 10 glasses a day. The best way to drink water is a glass before and after every meal and snack, rather than with the meal when it can dilute digestive functions.

<u>Healthy hint</u>- Fill a 2 quart container with water each morning and make sure it's all gone before 34 going to bed. Fiber and water are a dynamite duo!

What does fiber do for me?

1. Fiber increases in the diet have been found to lower blood pressures as much as 10% with no other dietary changes.

2. Those population groups with high fiber intakes have a low incidence of many different types of cancers, particularly colon cancer.

3. Fiber's bulky mass in the intestine promotes fullness. This, combined with the fact that high fiber foods take longer to eat and stay in the stomach longer, keep you full longer. This is good news for those interested in weight loss without hunger.

4. Fiber serves as a "time-release capsule," slowly and evenly releasing sugars from digested carbohydrates into the bloodstream. This keeps your energy levels even.

5. Fiber helps to protect against heart disease by lowering your level of "bad" LDL cholesterol.

6. Fiber regulates your G.I tract.

Be careful to add bran gradually; begin with 1 teaspoon oat bran and 1 teaspoon wheat bran and slowly increase as your body adjusts to more fiber. Both types of bran may be purchased from your grocery or natural food store.

7. It is important to choose whole grain foods at home to fill the void of what is missing in restaurants.

<u>Healthy goal</u>: Increase your fiber to keep your G.I tract regular, to help fight killer disease, to keep feeling full longer and to help you to say "no" to overeating by keeping your blood sugar level even.

Good health is everyone's major source of wealth. Without it, happiness is difficult.

How do I double my fiber?

1- Use whole grains such as brown rice, oats and WHOLE wheat rather than the white, refined types. When purchasing, look for words such as 100% whole wheat with the word "whole" first in the ingredient list. Many manufacturers call products whole grain even if they contain only minimal amounts of bran. Brown dye does wonders in making foods <u>look</u> healthy.

2- Eat vegetables and fruits with well washed skins on.

3- Choose more raw and lightly cooked vegetables but in as non-processed a form as possible. As a food becomes processed, ground, mashed, pureed or juiced, the fiber effectiveness is decreased.

4- Add a variety of legumes (dried beans and peanuts) to your diet.

5- Add unprocessed raw bran to your cereals. Raw oat bran (from oatmeal) is particularly useful in reducing cholesterol levels; raw wheat bran is particularly useful for a healthy, regular GI tract.

Refinement and Enrichment. A robbery that's legal.

Consider this story... A man was walking down the street when he was approached by a robber. The thief forced the man at gunpoint to take off all he was wearing - everything! After the man stripped, the thief said "I have just refined you." He then proceeded to return only four things; his watch, one shoe, his undershirt and necktie. The thief now proclaimed "I have just enriched you". Returning four nutrients and leaving out twenty one is what this enrichment thing is all about. A whole wheat berry contains approximately forty nutrients. When it is refined, every nutrient is affected and twenty one are completely lost. In the enrichment process, only four are added back. Don't be fooled by advertisements. White, even though it's enriched, is never nutritionally as good as whole grain.

5th Commandment:
Thou shalt trim the fat from your diet.

39

All about fat: On your body and on your plate

What is fat?

Fat is an essential nutrient needed in very limited amounts for lubrication of your body, for transporting fat-soluble vitamins and for fullness after eating. It is also a very concentrated way of getting calories and disease. Thinness does not give you the freedom to eat fat because thinness alone will not protect you from strokes and cancer. Trimming the excess fat from our diet goes far beyond fighting the fat on our body; it's choosing to make wise choices in our eating today to prevent the diseases of tomorrow.

Consider these vital facts about fat.

1. Excess fat intake increases your cholesterol and your risk of heart disease and stroke.
2. Excess fat intake increases your risk of cancer, particularly colon, prostate and breast cancer.
3. Excess fat increases your risk of gallbladder disease.
4. Excess fat, particularly saturated fat, has been shown to elevate blood pressure, regardless of the person's weight.

5. Excess fat fed to animals with a genetic susceptibility to diabetes made them far more likely to develop the disease. Those people with a family history of diabetes should consider cutting their fat intake as one step in prevention of this disease in their own life.

6. Excess fat intake helps make you fat! One ounce of fat supplies twice the number of calories as one ounce of carbohydrate or protein __and__ research shows that fat in food is stored as fat on the body much more readily than proteins or carbohydrates. It's not the bread and potatoes that give you those excess calories; it's the butter and cream sauces.

Healthy Hint - As a general rule, the thing that makes you fat is fat!

Foods high in saturated fats will raise your cholesterol level __four__ times faster than foods high in cholesterol.

41

Some Vital Definitions of Fat

<u>Cholesterol</u>: You need it but you don't have to eat it! It is necessary for many body functions, including hormone production, digestion, and efficient operation of the brain. But the body, in its infinite wisdom, produces all it needs. The liver produces cholesterol and those with a genetic tendency towards heart disease may have a liver that produces too much. It is not a vital nutrient you need to get from food.

Dangerous levels of cholesterol come from eating too much of the kind that comes from animal products such as meat, fish, chicken, eggs, milk, cheese and butter Or more commonly, it comes from a diet high in saturated fats which can convert to a bad form (LDL) of cholesterol.

When at high levels in the bloodstream, it tends to deposit in the walls of the blood vessels, especially those in the heart; leading to arteriosclerosis or "hardening of the arteries."

Cholesterol is produced in 2 major forms: H.D.L. (high density lipoprotein) and L.D.L. (low density lipoprotein.) H.D.L. (the good guys) protects the body by pulling the bad cholesterol, like a magnet, from the bloodstream, while L.D.L. is the substance that builds as plaque in the arteries.

<u>Triglycerides</u>: A type of fat whose function is to transport nutrients through the bloodstream but, when at high levels, will accumulate in blood vessels, similar to cholesterol, leading to the same increased risk of disease.

Triglycerides elevate from (1) high sugar, sweets, white flour products (refined carbohydrates) intake, (2) excess alcohol intake, (3) more commonly a pattern of nutrient overload. (Taking in most of your calories for the day at one time.) This is why 3 regular meals a day plus healthy snacks are very important.

43

Very Important Definitions of Oils

Saturated fat: includes all animal fats like butter, cream, poultry skin, bacon, sausage, cold cuts, hot dogs, marbling in meat as well as coconut and palm oil. It increases bad LDL cholesterol and the risk of disease.

Hydrogenation: Another hidden source of saturated fat is hydrogenated oils. In a manufacturing process called hydrogenation (used to make creamy products such as commercial peanut butter, non-dairy toppings and margarine) a polyunsaturated or monounsaturated oil is converted into a saturated oil. When buying a product, be sure that hydrogenated oil is not listed as one of the first three ingredients, as it is heart unhealthy.

Oil Definitions

<u>Monounsaturated fat</u>: found in olive, canola, and peanut oil. It increases 'good' HDL cholesterol and decreases bad LDL cholesterol and the risk of disease.

<u>Polyunsaturated fat</u>: includes all other vegetable oils such as safflower, corn, sesame, sunflower and cottonseed. It also includes avocado, almonds, pecans, walnuts. It decreases total cholesterol, both HDL's and LDL's.

<u>Omega 3 Fatty Acids</u> - EPA and DHA: Found in all fish, especially cold water fish, such as salmon and mackerel. These oils increase good (HDL) cholesterol while decreasing bad (LDL) cholesterol. They also decrease triglycerides and reduce the tendency of blood to form clots.

For A Healthier Heart

- Reduce Cholesterol Intake
- Avoid Saturated Fats
- Don't Smoke
- Exercise
- Eat High Fiber Foods
- Eat More Fish, Less Poultry and Meat
- Eat Onions and Garlic
- Lose Excess Body Fat

Exercise and Nutrition - The Fitness Connection

As vital as good nutrition is to total wellness, it is only one of the spokes in the wellness wheel. The proper combination of balanced eating and exercise is an unbeatable way to total wellbeing. Eat well to live well! Commitment to an exercise routine that goes hand-in-hand with good nutrition is one of the greatest gifts you can ever give yourself.

Ten Terrific Reasons to Exercise

1- Exercise increases your metabolism and decreases your appetite.

2- Exercise breaks the plateaus or "set points" of weight loss.

3- Exercise improves your quality of sleep. You fall asleep more quickly, sleep more soundly, wake up feeling more refreshed.

4- Exercise (if weight-bearing) will increase the density of the bones, preventing calcium loss and making them less prone to injury.

5- Exercise is nature's best tranquilizer. Activity disperses the hormones that accumulate during high-stress times. Mildly to moderately depressed people who exercise 15 to 30 minutes every other day will experience a positive mood swing in 3 weeks.

6- Exercise enhances your self-image. Those who exercise regularly feel better, more confident and in control of their lives than those who don't.

7- Exercise reduces your risk of chronic diseases. Non-exercisers are twice as likely to develop heart disease as those who exercise. The benefits occur from achieving that increased pulse rate and maintaining it for at least 20 minutes three times a week. Exercise helps in diabetes management making the cells more accepting of insulin. It regulates blood sugar, a major factor of reducing the risk of diabetes. Exercise helps to lower blood pressure. It also helps with arthritis management because exercise helps keep joints mobile.

8- Exercise improves your cholesterol profile. It increases levels of "good" cholesterol (HDL's) associated with a reduced risk of heart disease.

9- Exercise improves your mental capacity and slows the aging process. Many studies have shown that those who exercise have better reaction times, concentration levels and memory.

10- Exercise lowers your risk of getting certain cancers. Studies show that women who don't exercise have more than 2½ times the chance of developing cancer of the reproductive organs and almost twice the risk of getting breast cancer as those who exercise.

Exercise Guide to be F. I. T. T.

Frequency? 4 to 6 days a week

Intensity? At a level you feel slightly out of breath, without gasping. If something hurts, stop and rest. If the pain persists, check with your doctor. "No pain, no gain," is an exercise lie.

Time? 30 to 60 minutes, at a time of day you feel good and schedule allows a routine to be built.

Type? Whatever type of aerobic exercise you enjoy (or could enjoy) and can do regularly.

49

Rating the Fats
Meats, Fish, Poultry and Legumes

High Fat (8 or more grams per servings)	Medium Fat (4 to 7 grams per serving)	Low Fat (3 or fewer grams per serving)
bacon	beef (rib roast, steak)	chicken
commercial peanut-butter	eggs	clams
corned beef	ham	crab
duck	lamb chops	fish
frankfurters	pork chops	lean beef (flank, round)
goose	liver	legumes
ground meat	veal cutlet	oysters
luncheon meats		scallops
pepperoni		shrimp
sausage		tuna (water packed)
spareribs		
tuna, (oil packed)		

Rating the Fats
Dairy Foods

High Fat (8 or more grams per servings)	Medium Fat (4 to 7 grams per serving)	Low Fat (3 or fewer grams per serving)
Cheese: American blue Brie Camembert cheddar brick Swiss Cream-whipping half-and-half commercial sour whole milk whole milk yogurt	Cheese: farmer's feta mozzarella Light Philadelphia part-skim cheddar part-skim ricotta string cheese creamed cottage 2% milk	Cheese: low fat- cottage cheese Laughing Cow non-fat cheese non-fat ricotta 1% or skim milk non-fat plain yogurt

Rating the Fats
Sauces and Toppings

High Fat (8 or more grams per servings)	Medium Fat (4 to 7 grams per serving)	Low Fat (3 or fewer grams per serving)
avocado butter coconut mayonnaise margarine olives oils shortening nuts: almonds pecans cashews walnuts	salad dressings nuts: Brazil peanuts	light sour cream light mayonnaise no-oil salad dress- ing

Rating the Fats
Soups

High Fat (8 or more grams per servings)	Medium Fat (4 to 7 grams per serving)	Low Fat (3 or fewer grams per serving)
all creamed soups all chunky soups pea with ham	beef noodle black bean chicken noodle chicken vegetable	low-sodium chicken bouillon lentil vegetable vegetable bean gazpacho onion

Note: In commercial soups, even low-fat ones, notice the sodium content, as it is probably high.

♥ Super Substitutes ♥

Small steps that can make a big, fat difference!

♥ Use skim milk, non-fat plain yogurt, skim milk cheese, low fat cottage cheese and "light" cream cheese instead of higher fat dairy products.

♥ Cream soups are the most common ingredient in any casserole and the worst nutritionally. They can easily be replaced with chicken stock, wine or a combination, thickened with cornstarch or arrowroot. Add your own fresh mushrooms for a healthy cream of mushroom base that so many recipes call for. For an even richer base, combine non-fat dry milk with chicken stock and thicken with cornstarch or arrowroot.

♥ Cold skim evaporated milk with a touch of honey and vanilla is a super whipped topping. It does take longer to whip but the nutritional gains are worth it. You can also use 2 cups skim milk with one teaspoon lemon juice, chill well, then whip. Never use non-dairy whipped toppings. They are chemical non foods, loaded with saturated fat and sugar.

More Super Substitutes

♥ Basting with butter is another frustrating recipe direction for a healthy gourmet. Adapt instead by basting with tomato, lemon juice or stock.

♥ Use only <u>natural</u> peanut butter. Avoid commercial peanut butter! Commercial peanut butter is not much more than shortening and sugar but fresh ground peanut butter is a great source of protein. If you have trouble switching from the commercial type, begin by mixing it half and half with natural. Gradually increase the portion of natural.

♥ Try using legumes (dried beans and peas) as a main dish or a meat substitute for a high nutrition, low fat meal.

♥ Use canola or olive oil for salads or cooking. They are valuable sources of monounsaturated fat, but they are still fat so use sparingly.

Super Substitutes

♥ Purchase tuna packed in water rather than oil.

♥ Use non-stick sprays because they enable you to brown meats without grease.

♥ Dilute soy sauce or tamari sauce half and half with water and add 1 teaspoon lemon juice. It increases the flavor and reduces the salt. You may also use low sodium soy sauce.

♥ If using canned or frozen fruits, use only unsweetened, without sugar, packed in its own juices.

♥ Use more vanilla and spices in recipes. This will enable you to cut down more on the sugar since vanilla and spices enhance the impression of sweetness and flavor and have almost no calories.

♥ Healthy bread crumbs can be made by processing toasted, whole wheat bread in a food processor or blender.

More Super Substitutes

♥ Use whole grains anytime a recipe calls for white. Use brown rice or whole wheat pasta instead of white; whole grain crackers instead of saltines, etc.

♥ Substitute fiber and water for laxatives. A laxative isn't the healthy way to get rid of anything; fiber and water are!

♥ Use two egg whites in place of one whole egg. Egg whites are pure protein and egg yolks are pure fat. You may want to try some of the egg substitutes on the market now.

♥ Great potato toppings: salsa, nonfat sour cream, plain nonfat yogurt, blended till smooth nonfat cottage cheese, chives, grated parmesan.

6th Commandment: Thou shalt believe your mother was right: Eat your fruits and veggies.

6th Commandment: Thou shalt believe your Mother was right: **Eat your fruits and veggies.**

Vegetables provide a storehouse of vitamins, minerals and substances that serve as protectors against disease. They are also valuable sources of fiber and fluid. All in all, they are low calorie foods that make up an enormously important part of the healthy diet.

<u>Vegetables - Great cancer fighters!</u>

Research shows that the very substance that makes broccoli broccoli or cauliflower cauliflower has been found to have cancer-preventive characteristics. This substance is found in all vegetables belonging to the cruciferous family (cabbage, cauliflower, broccoli and Brussels sprouts). You should eat one of these cooked or raw everyday. A bonus is its vitamin C content. Research shows a daily intake of this vitamin blocks the action of certain body chemicals that could lead to cancer.

Beta-carotene, a nutrient found in fruits and vegetables has been shown to block the process by which a normal cell turns malignant and cancerous. Beta-carotene is what gives carrots, sweet potatoes, spinach, etc. their dark, rich coloring. This rich color in dark green leafy vegetables or in bright yellow-orange vegetables and fruits is the sign of the vegetables' storehouse of this valuable nutrient. The body converts beta-carotene to vitamin A in the digestive system. There is a safety valve attached in this conversion because the body will not convert it to vitamin A in toxic amounts. Eating these wonderful vegetables and fruits is the safe, miraculous way provided for us to attain Vitamin A.

Bringing nutritious foods home from the market is just the start. The way you cook them matters, too. Cooking affects not only the taste and appeal of food but also the nutritional value as well.

The best cooking techniques are: steaming, microwave cooking, stir-frying, poaching or broiling.

<u>Healthy goal:</u> Although people have developed toxicities from Vitamin A supplements, no one has ever died from an overdose of carrots, so remember that your mother really was right when she told you to "eat your veggies."

7th Commandment: Thou shalt get your vitamins from food, not pills.

Vitamins and Minerals · What are they anyway?

Vitamins are organic molecules that the body cannot do without, but does not produce on its own. They are chemical catalysts for the body; they make things happen! Vitamins <u>do not</u> give energy but they help the body to convert carbohydrates to energy and help the body use it. Any varied diet with enough calories should provide the essential vitamins and minerals the body needs. There is no need for the majority of people to take artificial vitamins, either in pill form or as part of "fortified" products. Rather than blanket supplementation, your goal should be to try to improve your eating pattern to assure adequate intake of all nutrients. The best source of vitamins and minerals is, and always has been, <u>FOOD!</u>

Who needs vitamin and mineral supplements?

Those at high risk of a vitamin deficiency are 1) chronic dieters whose intake gets cut along with the calories 2) those chronically ill, 3) heavy drinkers and smokers 4) pregnant or nursing mothers 5) those on special diets because of food allergies 6) those who have a limited intake of food choices. In these cases, a basic multi-vitamin/mineral supplement that supplies no more than 150% of the recommended daily allowance would be advised. A strict vegetarian eating only plant products also needs to supplement with vitamin B-12 which exists naturally only in animal foods.

Remember - You get <u>all</u> the fiber and 60% more vitamin C when you eat an orange instead of just drinking the juice.

The two categories of vitamins

Vitamins are either fat-soluble or water-soluble. Fat solubles are A,D,E,K. They are absorbed through the intestinal walls and can be stored in the body fat for long periods of time and because they accumulate in the body, you can more easily get into a toxic state from taking megadoses. Megadoses of vitamins are amounts that are more than 10 times the R.D.A (Recommended Daily Allowance). At best, they are a waste of money. At worst, they can be highly toxic. When you consider that your entire R.D.A. for vitamin A can be met through a cup of spinach or carrots every 5 days, the need for vitamins beyond that certainly needs to be questioned!

Water-soluble vitamins (B complex and C) cannot be stored in the body for long because they dissolve in water and are released in the urine.

Important facts to remember about vitamins.

No single food supplies your daily requirement of all the vitamins and minerals. The beautiful thing about good, balanced nutrition and the "Have It Your Way" Meal Plan is that everything fits together in such a perfect way that just focusing on these basic principles will allow an adequate intake of essential nutrients. You don't have to continually analyze your intake to be sure you've had your zinc.

8th Commandment: Thou shalt drink at least 8 glasses of water a day.

8th Commandment: Thou shalt drink at least eight glasses of water a day.

♥ Because water makes up 92% of our blood plasma, 80% of our muscle mass, 60% of our red blood cells and 50% of everything else in our body, water is vitally important for health. Water is as essential a nutrient as the other five: carbohydrates, proteins, fats, vitamins, and minerals.

♥ As you begin to drink water, your natural thirst for it will increase and as you learn about all that water does, your motivation for drinking it will grow as well. Water drinking is habit-forming; the more you drink, the more you want.

Why is water so essential?

♥ Water is essential for preventing excess fluid retention. Water is the natural diuretic. It is the best way to get rid of excess fluid.

♥   Water is essential for allowing proper bowel function. Water is the only liquid you consume that doesn't require the body to work to metabolize it or excrete it but will freely move through the GI tract. Water, with the juice of a lemon, first thing in the morning makes a great waker-upper for your GI tract. It aids in digestion and acts as a mild, natural laxative.

♥ Water is essential for maintaining proper muscle tone. Water gives muscles their natural ability to contract and prevent dehydration. It also works to keep the skin healthy and resilient.

♥ Water is essential for helping to rid the body of waste. Water is the vehicle that the body must have to flush out the waste produced in normal body functions.

♥ Water is a wonderful, natural appetite depressant. Drinking a full glass of water before and after each meal and snack will allow you to be satisfied with much less food.

How much water do I need?

You need 8 to 10 glasses of water each day. Do not rely on your thirst mechanism; it will only replace about 35 to 40% of your needs. Also, don't rely on your intake of other liquids. <u>No</u> other liquid can work like water. If you do not take in adequate water, your body fluids will be thrown out of balance and you may experience fluid retention, constipation, unexplained weight gain and loss of that natural thirst mechanism. Begin to focus on drinking wonderful, essential water and be sure to drink enough.

If you are drinking tap water, you may find the taste will improve with refrigeration for 24 hours (the chlorine dissipates). Water is refreshing with lemon or lime slices added and bottled water, club soda or seltzer water is a nice treat.

9th Commandment: Thou shalt use a minimum of salt, sugar, caffeine and alcohol.

9th Commandment: Thou shalt use a minimum of salt, sugar, caffeine and alcohol.

All of the "Commandments of Healthy Eating" up to this point have focused on the nutrients vital to wellness. This commandment points to the need to avoid some things which do not benefit the body but rather can cause serious detriment if taken to excess. The problem with salt, sugar, caffeine and alcohol is that they can easily cause a problem with overindulgence. If you are a person that may be taking in any or all of these substances to excess, if you have the "more you have, the more you want" syndrome, this commandment is for you!

Salt - <u>Don't</u> Pass It!

"Please pass the salt" is a common phrase which is overused by most Americans. We need to shake the habit! The taste for salt is conditioned, and as you begin to use less of it, your tastes will change so that you will enjoy foods more without it. Be patient with yourself and your family but begin to gradually cut back on your use of salt in cooking and eliminate completely those snacks that are triple threats: high in salt, fat and calories.

What is salt?

Its chemical name is sodium chloride... with sodium being the more important in terms of health. Everyone requires some sodium but there's more than enough naturally present in foods to supply this requirement. Most of us consume 5 to 25 times more than we need.

73

Effects of Salt

Excessive sodium is indicated in many diseases, with the most prevalent being hypertension and kidney disease. Excess salt causes temporary buildup of body fluids in your system. This makes it more difficult for your heart to pump blood through the cardiovascular system and the results may be high blood pressure. It's wise to practice prevention and begin to cut back on its excess in your eating.

Great Substitutes for Salt

Where do I get sodium and how can I shake the habit?

1. Cutting back on your use of more highly processed foods and salty snacks will substantially reduce your sodium intake.

2. Leave the salt shaker off the table. You'll quickly begin to enjoy the natural flavor of your food without covering them with salt. Try substituting herbs and spices for some of the salt.

3. Attempt to cook with herb blends rather than salt to add new flavors to cooking. Try making your own and keep in a large holed shaker right by the stove where your salt used to be.
   <u>Seasoning blends</u>: (I) 2 tsp. dry mustard, 1½ tsp. oregano, 1 tsp. marjoram, 1 tsp. thyme, 1 tsp. garlic powder, 1 tsp. curry powder, ½ tsp. onion powder, ½ tsp. celery seed. (II) 1 Tbs. garlic powder, 1 Tbs. dry mustard, 1 Tbs. paprika, 1½ tsp. pepper, 1 tsp. basil, ½ tsp. thyme.

4. Watch out for these high sodium foods :

- ♥ Any food pickled or brine cured, like **sauerkraut, pickles**.
- ♥ Any food salt-cured or smoked, like ham and bacon.
- ♥ Salted snack foods like salted top crackers and chips.
- ♥ Condiments, like soy sauce and ketchup. Use in moderation.
- ♥ Convenience foods, like frozen dinners and instant soup mix.
- ♥ Most canned foods like canned soups, vegetable juices, canned vegetables. Check label for sodium content.

Cheer up! Sodium does not have to be cut out completely; you only need to be aware of its sources and begin to cut back on excess use. Accept the challenge of learning to cook and enjoy foods without the usual added fat and salt. Included are many wonderful recipes that are a great place to start.

Those that loaf have no bread!

Sugar: How sweet it isn't!

Sugar is called by many names - honey, brown sugar, corn syrup, fructose, etc, but it's all sugar! Occasional use of sugar is possible for some but impossible for others. Those that are very sensitive to blood sugar fluctuations will be hurt by "just a little bit" not by calories, but by the effect it has on their body. The "seesaw effect" that sugar has seems to result in a "more you have, more you want" addiction. A heavy sugar intake causes a quick rise in blood sugar that will be followed by a quick fall. That dip in blood sugar triggers "eating for a lift" to relieve fatigue. Usually the food is, again, high in sugar and the "seesaw effect" continues!

Sugar has been shown to cause dental cavities, obesity, and high triglycerides as well as wreaking havoc in the control of diabetes and hypoglycemia.

Sugary foods may be replacing other healthier foods (such as fruit) which would contribute vitamins, minerals and fiber.

Most high sugar snacks (candy bars, cookies, donuts, etc.) are also loaded with saturated fats and calories - another triple threat to good health.

<u>Healthy Goal</u>: Cut back on your daily use of sugar or sweets and eat fruit to satisfy your natural craving for sugar. Sugar is not worth robbing yourself of your precious energy and stamina.

Anyone can count the seeds in an apple but only God can count the apples in a seed.

Artificial Sweeteners - Good or Bad?

There are no absolutes in the safety of chemicals, be it saccharin or aspartame or any new one to come. The final results of its use will not be in for years. As bad as sugar is and the health hazards indicated in its overuse, at least it's not chemical and it's been used for centuries.

Understand that as long as you continue to use sugar laden foods or sugar substitutes, you will keep your taste buds alive for sugar. The goal is to begin to cut back on its use so that the need is not there for everything to have to taste sweet; to allow your taste buds to change so that the desire for sweetness can be met in a safer way. Try fruits and other naturally sweet foods that are God's natural provision for our inborn sweet preference.

Healthy Goal: When in doubt, leave it out!

79

Breaking the caffeine habit

What is caffeine and how does it affect me?

A relatively mild stimulant, caffeine is among the worlds most widely used and addictive drugs. Some using even small amounts of it may suffer side effects such as restlessness and disturbed sleep, palpitations of the heart, stomach irritation, fibro-cystic breast disease and diarrhea. The amount required to cause a stimulant effect is estimated to be about 150-250 mg, the amount in 1 to 2 cups of brewed coffee. This is not a lot of coffee.

Here is a brief reminder on the major sources:

<u>Coffee</u>: The amount of caffeine in coffee depends on a number of factors, how it's brewed and how long, whether it's regular ground or instant. Decaf brands, of course, just have a few milligrams of caffeine per cup. Many "withdrawers" do well to come off slowly by brewing ½ decaf and ½ caffeinated as their body adjusts. Be sure to try the "Swiss-water processed decafs; they come in flavored varieties

80

that are especially wonderful and are decaffeinated without chemicals. They can be found at most specialty coffee and tea shops as well as certain grocery or department stores.

<u>Tea</u>: It will typically have about 1/3 the caffeine of a cup of brewed coffee, the longer it brews the higher the caffeine level. There are also a number of decaffeinated teas available.

<u>Sodas</u>: Generally, the cola beverages will have the highest levels of caffeine but look at labels to be sure that your favorite fruit variety does not contain it. Some orange and lemon drinks have as much as coffee.

<u>Chocolate</u>: Chocolate drinks and candies also contain caffeine due to the high caffeine level of the cocoa bean. The caffeine content of hot chocolate is usually 1/4 a cup of brewed coffee. One oz. of baking chocolate contains 1/3 the caffeine in a cup of coffee.

<u>Over the Counter Drugs:</u> Read labels carefully! Stimulants such as No-Doz, Vivarin and even some headache relievers supply as much caffeine as 2 cups of regular coffee.

Our problem isn't not knowing what is right, it is doing it.

Don't Mix Alcohol with Wellness

People seem to be getting the idea that being healthy and fit is a good thing.

Alcohol is one of the most common and addictive drugs of our time. The U.S.D.A. Dietary Guidelines suggest "if you drink alcoholic beverages, do so in moderation and don't drive". What is considered moderate? One light beer, 4 oz. wine or 1½ oz. of liquor a day is acceptable but the minute you drink more, your health hazards escalate.

This recommendation comes from much medical research that implicates excess alcohol as a major risk factor in many killer diseases: cancer, cirrhosis and fatty liver, and congestive heart failure. Cirrhosis of the liver is now the fastest growing illness in the U.S. Alcohol is also the number one cause of malnutrition.

There is increasing evidence about the effect of alcohol consumption by pregnant women and on their developing babies. Studies have shown that babies born to mothers that drink have lower IQ's and higher rates of heart and joint defects. Even babies born to mothers that drink in moderation have been shown to be affected negatively. It is for this reason that pregnant women are usually advised _not_ to drink, even in small amounts. When in doubt, leave it out!

The Good News About Alcohol!

Americans are beginning to drink less; they are limiting themselves to one drink and making that one light. They are also getting more and more upset about drunken drivers and this is cutting back on overall liquor sales.

Healthy Goal: Reduce or eliminate alcohol consumption. The effects of alcohol tend to suppress discipline as well as the appetite control center. Drinking sets you up for excessive eating and undisciplined behavior.

Healthy Hints for Good Nutrition

♥ Never eat "all you can eat" at "all you can eat" restaurants. This also means brunches, covered dish dinners, etc.

♥ Try not to have more than 2 cups of beverages containing caffeine per day. In addition to the health risk, the caffeine will stimulate your appetite.

♥ Eat the fruit and veggies on your plate first. They cause a quicker rise in your blood sugar and will make you feel full quicker.

♥ Eat slowly! It takes 20 minutes for your brain to get the message that your stomach is satisfied. Dine, don't eat!

♥ Warm foods are more satisfying than cold. The cold stimulates more gastric acid to be produced and will not satisfy, but often intensifies, hunger.

♥ The best beverage you can drink to replace fluid after exercise is and always has been, WATER.

♥ Always have your snack handy. Plan ahead so you won't be tempted to reach for the wrong foods 85

♥ Leave the salt shaker OFF the table to break the 'salt before you taste' habit.

♥ Try to stay out of tempting territory. Don't buy problem foods and unhealthy snacks. A glimpse of a tempting food is enough to alert your brain mechanism and start your gastic juices flowing. If you must buy them, keep them out of sight.

♥ Never go to the grocery store hungry. Eat first, shop later. Take a grocery list and stick to it.

♥ Recognize that television advertisements are not in the least concerned with your health or long life. Don't let them tempt you to buy something that is not healthy. Read labels instead.

♥ All alcoholic beverages are loaded with empty calories and have absolutely no nutritional value.

♥ Laxatives are not a healthy way to get rid of anything. Fiber and water are! Try a glass of warm water and the juice of a lemon first thing in the morning. It is a mild, natural laxative.

♥ Choose crunchy foods over soft foods. Psychologically, we need to chew; it releases stress and tension.

♥ Putting food in a body that doesn't need it is just the same as putting it in a trashcan. The difference is that it doesn't hurt the trashcan.

♥ Total health is never destroyed by one extravagant meal, one hot dog at a ball game or one birthday cake. Don't give up and quit the race; get back on track right away. There is no amount of falling down that can stop the runner determined to finish.

The mark of wise people is their ability to distinguish a setback from defeat.

Super Quick Weight Loss Diet

Gotcha, Didn't I !!!

Go back to the introduction and begin to read! By the time you get here again, you will know there are <u>NO</u> quick-fix ways of losing weight for a lifetime! But you really know that already, don't you? It hasn't worked so far – and it never will. So it's time to break the diet mentality with a nutritional plan that works for life. You <u>can</u> feel better, have abundant energy from morning till night and look more radiant and healthy. <u>You</u> are in charge. <u>You</u> can change. Now that you have a new plan of eating, wellness can be yours!

If at first you don't succeed –
try reading the directions.

10th Commandment: Thou shalt never go on a fad diet.

10th Commandment: Thou shalt never go on a fad diet.

Why is it so easy to gain weight and so hard to lose? Why is it so hard to keep off.? What is the answer? It begins by choosing a way of eating and living, a nutrition plan for a lifetime, <u>Never A Diet!</u> The way you choose to eat to lose weight must be livable and comfortable enough that you can stay with it the rest of your life. My "Have It Your Way" plan gives you this new way of life; losing weight as a side effect of your eating better and keeping every pound off because you have no reason to go back to your old way of eating. Stop setting yourself up for a starvation-gorge way of existence while your weight goes up and down like a yo-yo.

Ultra-low calorie intake is self-defeating. The body simply slows down to avoid starvation and dramatic weight loss.

Stop looking at weight loss as a punishment of eating awful tasting and worse looking foods or swallowing pills. A way of eating for life will not have you exclude any major food group or nutrient, nor will it warn you against going on it for more than 2 weeks.

The most wonderful thing about this meal plan is that you don't have to carry a book on calories in food everywhere you go; you only need to focus on eating healthy foods at the right time.

This nutrition plan is a new way of eating, providing you with a lifetime of high energy and wellness. Don't be discouraged if you don't immediately see the pounds drop or if you hit a plateau; remember, this is not a fad diet!

The task ahead of you is never as great as the power behind you. You have been created with a genetic heritage for wellness. Claim that power!

You'll wonder how you can eat so much so often and still lose weight!

"HAVE IT YOUR WAY" WEIGHT LOSS MEAL PLAN FOR WOMEN

BREAKFAST —(within 1/2 hour of arising)

COMPLEX CARBO:	1 slice whole wheat toast OR 1/2 English Muffin/bagel OR 1 homemade muffin OR 3/4 cup cereal (with added bran)
PROTEIN:	1 oz. lowfat cheese or 1/4 cup lowfat cottage cheese OR 1 egg (only 3 times/wk) or 1/4 cup egg substitute OR 3/4 cup skim milk or nonfat yogurt for cereal
SIMPLE CHO:	1 small fresh fruit

MORNING SNACK

CARBOHYDRATE:	1 small fresh fruit OR 3 whole grain crackers OR 1 rice cake or Wasa
PROTEIN:	1 oz. part-skim or fat free cheese OR lean meat OR 1/2 cup nonfat yogurt OR 1/4 cup lowfat cottage cheese

LUNCH

SIMPLE CHO:	1 small fresh fruit
COMPLEX CARBO:	2 slices bread OR 1 small baked potato OR 1 whole wheat pita
PROTEIN:	2 oz. (cooked poultry, fish, seafood, lean beef or lowfat cheese) OR 1/2 cup cooked legumes
HEALTHY MUNCHIES:	Raw vegetables as desired (up to 2 cups) with lemon juice, vinegar, mustard or no-oil salad dressing
ADDED FAT: (optional)	1 Tbsp. light mayonnaise OR 1 tsp. oil OR 1 Tbsp. salad dressing

92

DINNER

SIMPLE CHO:	1 small fresh fruit OR 1 cup nonstarchy vegetables
COMPLEX CARBO:	1/2 cup rice or pasta OR 1/2 cup starchy vegetables
PROTEIN:	2 to 3 oz. cooked skinless poultry, seafood, fish, lean beef OR 1/2 cup cooked legumes
HEALTHY MUNCHIES: **(optional)**	Raw vegetables (up to 2 cups) as desired with lemon juice, vinegar, or no-oil salad dressing
ADDED FAT: **(optional)**	May use 1 tsp. olive or canola oil OR 1 Tbsp. salad dressing OR 1 tsp. butter or margarine

NIGHT SNACK—1 small fresh fruit OR 3 cups microwave light popcorn OR 1/2 cup cereal with 1/2 cup skim milk

The right attitude puts you on the path to healthful eating. Rather than focusing on foods to avoid, think instead about adding new, good foods. You'll feel satisfied, not deprived and you'll be so full of the best foods that you won't want the ones that drag you down.

93

Great news! You won't be deprived of lots of good food.

"HAVE IT YOUR WAY" WEIGHT MAINTENANCE MEAL PLAN FOR WOMEN AND WEIGHT LOSS MEAL PLAN FOR MEN

BREAKFAST —(within 1/2 hour of arising)

SIMPLE CHO: 1 small fresh fruit

COMPLEX CARBO: 2 slices whole wheat toast OR 1 English Muffin/bagel OR 2 homemade muffins OR 1 1/2 cups cereal (with added bran)

PROTEIN: 2 oz. lowfat cheese or 1/2 cup lowfat cottage cheese OR 2 eggs (only 2 times/wk) or 1/2 cup egg substitute OR 1 1/2 cups skim milk or nonfat yogurt for cereal

MORNING SNACK

CARBOHYDRATE: 1 fresh fruit OR 5 whole grain crackers OR 2 rice cakes or Wasa OR 1 slice whole wheat bread

PROTEIN: 2 oz. part-skim or fat free cheese OR lean meat OR 1 cup nonfat yogurt OR 1/2 cup lowfat cottage cheese

LUNCH

SIMPLE CHO:
COMPLEX CARBO:
PROTEIN:

1 fresh fruit
2 slices bread OR 1 baked potato OR 1 whole wheat pita
3 oz. (cooked poultry, fish, seafood, lean beef or lowfat cheese) OR 3/4 cup cooked legumes

HEALTHY MUNCHIES:
(optional)
ADDED FAT:
(optional)

Raw vegetables as desired (up to 2 cups) with lemon juice, vinegar, mustard or no-oil salad dressing
1 Tbsp. light mayonnaise OR 1 tsp. oil OR 1 Tbsp. salad dressing

94

AFTERNOON SNACK —Repeat earlier snack choices OR 1/4 cup Trail Mix (page 18)

DINNER
SIMPLE CHO: 1 fresh fruit OR 1 cup nonstarchy vegetables
COMPLEX CARBO: 1 cup rice or pasta OR 1 cup starchy vegetables
PROTEIN: 3 to 4 oz. cooked skinless poultry, seafood, fish, lean beef OR 1 cup cooked legumes
HEALTHY MUNCHIES: Raw vegetables (up to 2 cups) as desired with lemon juice, vinegar, or no-oil
(optional) salad dressing
ADDED FAT: May use 1 tsp. olive or canola oil OR 1 Tbsp. salad dressing OR 1 tsp. butter or
(optional) margarine

NIGHT SNACK—1 fresh fruit OR 3 cups microwave light popcorn OR 3/4 cup cereal with 1/2 cup
skim milk

At your ideal weight, the maintenance meal plan will allow you to keep your weight at the perfect place for life.

95

"HAVE IT YOUR WAY" WEIGHT MAINTENANCE MEAL PLAN FOR MEN

BREAKFAST —(within 1/2 hour of arising)

SIMPLE CHO: 2 servings fresh fruit

COMPLEX CARBO: 2 slice whole wheat toast OR 1 English Muffin/bagel OR 2 homemade muffins AND 3/4 cup cereal (with added bran)

PROTEIN: 2 oz. lowfat cheese or 1/2 cup lowfat cottage cheese OR 2 eggs (only 2 times/wk) or 1/2 cup egg substitute OR 1 1 /2 cups skim milk or nonfat yogurt

MORNING SNACK

CARBOHYDRATE: 1 fresh fruit AND 5 whole grain crackers OR 2 rice cake or Wasa OR 1 slice whole wheat bread

PROTEIN: 2 oz. part-skim or fat free cheese OR lean meat OR 1 cup nonfat yogurt OR 1/2 cup lowfat cottage cheese

LUNCH

SIMPLE CHO: 2 servings fresh fruit

COMPLEX CARBO: 2 slices bread OR 1 baked potato OR 1 whole wheat pita

PROTEIN: 3-4 oz. (cooked poultry, fish, seafood, lean beef or lowfat cheese) OR 1 cup cooked legumes

HEALTHY MUNCHIES: Raw vegetables as desired (up to 2 cups) with lemon juice, vinegar, mustard or **(optional)** no-oil salad dressing

ADDED FAT: 1 Tbsp. light mayonnaise OR 1 tsp. oil OR 1 Tbsp. salad dressing **(optional)**

96

<u>AFTERNOON SNACK</u>—Repeat earlier snack choices OR 1/2 cup Trail Mix (page 18)

<u>DINNER</u>

SIMPLE CHO:	1 fresh fruit AND 1 cup nonstarchy vegetables
COMPLEX CARBO:	1 1/2 cups rice or pasta OR 1 1/2 cups starchy vegetables
PROTEIN:	3 to 4 oz. cooked skinless poultry, seafood, fish, lean beef OR 1 cup cooked legumes
HEALTHY MUNCHIES: **(optional)**	Raw vegetables (up to 2 cups) as desired with lemon juice, vinegar, or no-oil salad dressing
ADDED FAT: **(optional)**	May use 1 tsp. olive or canola oil OR 1 Tbsp. salad dressing OR 1 tsp. butter or margarine

<u>NIGHT SNACK</u>—1 cup cereal with 1 cup skim milk or nonfat yogurt AND 1 serving fruit

GROCERY LIST
GRAINS

100% Whole Wheat Bread —look for "whole" as first word of ingredient list

Whole Wheat Bagels, English Muffins, Hamburger Buns and Pita bread

Whole Wheat Pasta (best variety at Natural Food Store)

Whole Wheat Pastry Flour (best for muffins, pancakes, etc.) at Natural Food Store

Brown Rice, Instant Brown Rice, and Wild Rice

Whole Grain Crackers and Such

    Crispbread - Wasa (2=1 Complex Carbo) and Kavli (4=1 Complex Carbo)

    Crispy Cakes (2=1 Complex Carbo)

    Guiltless Gourmet No Oil Tortilla Chips (1 oz. = 1 Complex Carbo)

    Harvest Crisp (5=1 Complex Carbo)

    Mini-Rice Cakes (4=1 Complex Carbo)

    Rice Cakes (2=1 Complex Carbo)

    Ry-Krisp (3=1 Complex Carbo)

Great Cereals—(Generally, 3/4 cup = 1 Complex Carbo)

    Cheerios (General Mills)

    Grape-Nuts (concentrated; 1/4 cup=1 Complex Carbo)

    Muesli (Ralston)

    Nutrigrain Almond-Raisin or Wheat (Kellogg's)

    Puffed Rice, Puffed Wheat (Lightweight; 1 cup=1 Complex Carbo)

    Oatmeal, Oat Bran

    Raisin Squares (Kellogg's)

    Shredded Wheat, Shredded Wheat 'N Bran (Nabisco)

    Unprocessed Wheat Bran

    Wheatena

DAIRY AND DELI

<u>Cheese</u> (lowfat= less than 5 grams fat per ounce)
    Alpine Lace "Lean and Free"
    Cottage Cheese (Fat Free or 1%)
    Cream Cheese (Kraft "Light" Tub or Fat Free, Healthy Choice Fat Free)
    Farmer's
    Jarlsberg Lite
    Kraft Light Naturals
    Mozzarella (Nonfat, Part-skim or String Cheese)
    Parmesan (fresh grated)
    Ricotta (Nonfat or Part-skim)
    String Cheese - try MooTown Snackers Light
    The Laughing Cow Reduced Calorie (needs no refrigeration)
    Weight Watcher's Natural
<u>Eggs or Egg Substitutes</u>
<u>Milk</u> (Skim or 1% lowfat)
<u>Margarine (Fleischmann's Squeeze is best) or Butter</u>
<u>Nonfat Plain Yogurt</u> (may add all-fruit jam to sweeten)
<u>Stonyfield Farms Nonfat Yogurt</u> (sweetened with fruit and fruit juice)

MISCELLANEOUS

Assorted variety of seasonal fresh fruits and vegetables;
   DON'T FORGET: bananas, apples, oranges, melon, strawberries,
   romaine lettuce, broccoli, carrots, tomatoes, squash, white and
   sweet potatoes. Also buy raisins and canned, unsweetened applesauce,
   crushed pineapple.

Mayonnaise - May use a tsp. of traditional mayonnaise OR
   1 Tbsp. Miracle Whip Lite OR Kraft Light and Lively OR Hellman's Light
   (Believe it or not, light mayo is healthier than fat free - it has less chemicals
   and sugar)
Olive oil, Canola oil

Natural Peanut Butter
   May buy fresh ground at deli OR from health food store

Popcorn - Orville Redenbacher's Light Natural Microwave OR Pop Weaver Light

Dry roasted, unsalted peanuts and shelled sunflower seeds

Low Calorie Salad Dressings

   May prefer to use 1 Tbsp. regular dressing with lemon juice OR
   vinegar
   Bernstein's Low Calorie Cheese Italian OR Vinegarette; Pritikin;
   Kraft "No Oil" Dressing; Barendorf's

No Sugar Jam - try Sorrell Ridge, Polaner Preserves or Smuckers
   Simply Fruit (Fruit Only Preserves) OR Welch's Totally Fruit

Your survival kit for staying Alive and Well in the Fast Food Lane!

SURVIVAL TIPS

You must be aware of the "hidden fats" in restaurant prepared foods and must never be timid about ordering foods in a "special style." You are paying (and paying well!) for the meal and service, and deserve to have foods prepared the way you desire. You also deserve to know the "content" of what you are going to eat! LEARN TO BE DISCRIMINATING, NOT INTIMIDATED!

1. Think BEFORE you order!

2. Order meats, fish or poultry broiled or grilled without butter, sauces <u>on the side</u>. Good choices: petite filet, marinated breast of chicken, broiled fish or seafood, and steamed shellfish.

3. Entrees that are poached in wine or lemon juice are acceptable as well as those simmered in tomato sauces.

4. When fresh vegetables are available, order them steamed without sauces or butter.

5. You may also have a slice of bread or dinner roll as a complex carbohydrate.

6. A baked potato is the best choice for your carbohydrate, even a better choice than the rice pilaf that is usually sauteed in fat. (Ask for a substitution.) Ask for sour cream or butter <u>on the side</u>. A side dish of pasta with red sauce is a refreshing alternative to the potato; watch your portion.

7. Fresh fruit is a good substitution for your cooked vegetables (sometimes difficult to get in a restaurant). Fruit is many times served as an appetizer but they will serve it as dessert. (It is a much healthier choice than mousse!)

8. All salads must have dressing <u>on the side</u>! Uf you use dressing, lightly use 1 Tbsp. for taste with additional vinegar and lemon juice for moistness.

9. Remember to always have a carbohydrate and a protein source, never just a salad alone. You may order a chef's salad with extra turkey rather than ham, or a shrimp cocktail with your salad, just be sure to provide yourself with a protein. Your carbohydrate may be a roll, crackers or baked potato.

10. Never eat all you can eat at all-you-can-eat brunches, restaurants, or covered dish dinners. Your overeating ("I want to get my money's worth") is not going to cheat the restaurant out of anything, but can cheat you out of many healthy years!

11. Menus are filled with clues about what their foods contain. AVOID THESE WORDS:

A LA MODE (with ice cream)
AU FROMAGE (with cheese)
AU GRATIN (in cheese sauce)
AU LAIT (with milk)
BASTED (with extra fat)
BISQUE (cream soup)
BUTTERED (with extra fat)
CASSEROLE (with extra fat)
CREAMED (with extra fat)
CRISPY (means fried)
ESCALLOPED (with cream sauce)
PAN-FRIED (fried with extra fat)
HASH (with extra fat)
HOLLANDAISE (with cream sauce)
SAUTEED (fried with extra fat)

If you see these words in the description of an appealing entree, be bold enough to ask for the entree prepared in a special way, i.e. if the description says "Buttered," ask for it without added butter; if the description says "Pan-Fried," ask for it grilled or poached instead.

12. Remember, it's your money, your health, and your waistline! Speak up. Don't be intimidated!

SOME SUGGESTIONS FOR DINING OUT HEALTHFULLY

MEXICAN — always order <u>ala carte</u> (refried beans are made with pure lard). Order a salad to be served immediately with dressing on the side. The salad will prevent "eat because they're there" munching on the chips. And beware of the Margaritas—they are loaded with both salt and sugar, to say nothing of the alcohol!

Ideas: Black Bean Soup, Chili, or Gazpacho, Chicken Burrito, Tostada, or Enchilada, Soft Chicken Tacos, Chicken Fajitas (without added fat)

ORIENTAL — order dishes that have been <u>lightly stir</u> fried (not deep fried like egg rolls) without heavy gravies or sweet and sour sauces. Eat <u>1/2 portion</u> served with <u>steamed</u> rice; do not use fried. Many restaurants will prepare food without MSG if you ask, and be careful to watch the soy sauce you add. Both are loaded with sodium! All items can be acceptable for the bold sodium watcher who asks for neither soy sauce nor MSG!

Ideas: Bamboo-steamed vegetables with chicken, seafood or fish
Moo Goo Gai Pan, Shrimp or Tofu with vegetables (with no MSG and little oil)
Won ton, hot and sour or miso soup, Udon with meat and vegetables

ITALIAN - portion size control is important here; the typical plate full of spaghetti is 5 times too much!! You will do much better with a side dish or appetizer portion. Always order salad with dressing on the side, and never hesitate to ask for a red sauce rather than a butter or white sauce.

Ideas: *Lasagna (have approximately a 3" x 5" piece)
           Canneloni
           *Grilled chicken with pasta side dish or bread
           *Fresh fish with pasta side dish or bread
           *Clams Linquine with Red Sauce (careful with
           amounts of pasta eaten!)
           *Minestrone Soup and Salad, dressing on side; ala
           carte mozzarella cheese or meatballs for protein.
           *Side dish of spaghetti with 2 ala carte meatballs
           *Grilled Shrimp on Fettucine with Red Sauce
*Lower sodium choice - have with slice of bread rather
than pasta with red sauce.

STEAK HOUSES - Portion control is also crucial here. A 16 oz. steak or prime rib will give you 5 times more than needed. Order the smallest cut available and don't be fearful of taking some home! Lowest sodium choice is filet or london broil without salt.

Ideas: Petite Cut Filet, Shish-Ka-Bob or Brochette
           Slices of London Broil (no sauces, please!)
           Hawaiian Chicken, Charbroiled Shrimp

SEAFOOD - order fish/seafood when possible, steamed, boiled, grilled or broiled <u>without butter</u>. A small amount of cocktail sauce is a better choice for dipping than butter (2 dips in butter = 50 calories). Remember small seafood items such as shrimp, oysters etc. are "deadly" in terms of fat and calories when fried; the surface area is so high, more breading adheres and absorbs more fat. All can be low sodium choices when grilled and if sauces are avoided.

Ideas: Fresh Fish of the Day - Grilled when possible, without butter and sauce to the side
Steamed oysters, shrimp, or clams (5 = 1 oz. protein)
Lobster/Crabmeat/Crab Claws (1/4 cup = 1 oz. protein)
Seafood Kabobs, Mesquite grilled shrimp
Blackened Fish prepared without butter (high sodium)

APPETIZER HEAVENS - Many restaurants specialize in appetizers: Fried Cheese, Nachos, Fried Potato Skins "loaded" with bacon, sour cream and cheese, fried zucchini and mushrooms. These are cardiovascular nightmares when you consider 2 potato skins OR 2 pieces of fried cheese are basically the fat calories of a whole meal (and should be used as such!). Many restaurants are offering raw vegetable platters; vegetables are safe but not the dip, so very, very carefully indulge!

Good choices: Chicken burritos or fajitas, Grilled Seafood
Marinated chicken breast, Non-creamed Soup

<u>HEALTH/NATURAL FOOD RESTAURANTS</u> - do not feel "safe" here <u>by any means</u>! Although you will have an opportunity to get whole grains and nicer fresh vegetable salads, the fats and sodium come in even more deceptively! Beware of sauces and high fat cheeses smothering the foods, and high fat dressings on salads and sandwiches. Many foods are prepared in the same way as at the Fast Food Restaurant, they just have healthier sounding names. You can do well here, however, with judicious choices. Again, the salads and salad bars are lovely, just follow the same guideline of dressing to the side and its minimal use. If you have a cheese dish, be sure to use no other added fats in the meal; the cheese will contain enough for the day!

Good choices: Vegetable Soup and 1/2 sandwich (avoid tuna/chicken salad due to mayo)
"Chef" type salad and whole grain roll (no ham)
Stir fry dishes asking for "light" on oil
Marinated breast of chicken
Fresh fish of the day - grilled when possible
Vegetable Omelet with whole grain roll
Pitas stuffed with vegetables and cheese
Fruit plate with plain yogurt/cottage cheese
and whole grain roll

<u>BREAKFAST OUT</u> — Breakfast can be a special meal out due to such safe and easy choices. If breakfast is later than normal, have a snack when first arising, then the later meal. You also may choose to have your larger lunch portions for breakfast, and a smaller lunch 3 to 4 hours later. Follow these guidelines in ordering:

1. Be sure to always order whole wheat toast or grits <u>unbuttered</u>; you may add one teaspoon of butter, if desired.

2. You are usually safer to order a la carte so that you are not paying for, or tempted by, the abundance of food in the "breakfast specials" or buffets.

3. Be bold and creative in ordering! Rather than accepting French toast with syrup and bacon; ask for it made with whole wheat bread, no syrup and a side dish of fresh berries or fruit instead. Many restaurants will substitute cottage cheese or 1 egg for the meat. Many restaurants also serve oatmeal and cereal even though it's not always on the menu. It's a nice carbohydrate with milk and fresh fruit, especially strawberries or blueberries.

4. Always look for a protein <u>and</u> a carbohydrate source. A Danish doesn't do it!

> **Good choices:** Eggs and whole wheat toast or English muffin
> French Toast with berries
> Fresh vegetable omelet and toast
> Cereal with skim milk and fruit
> Fresh fruit bowl with cottage cheese and
>   whole wheat toast

HEALTHIER "FAST FOOD"

As in any experience with dining out, the healthy "fast food gourmet" must be aware of the hidden fats in foods ordered.

* SPECIAL SAUCES: "NOT-SO-SPECIAL" FAT AND SODIUM! It's the mayonnaise, special sauces, sour cream, etc. that triples the fat, sodium and calories in fast foods; always order your food without them!

* Stuffed potatoes may seem a healthy addition to the fast food menu but not with the cheese sauces they are smothered in — equivalent to 9 PATS OF BUTTER PER POTATO! Ask for grated cheese with no butter, instead.

* Chicken is truly a lowfat alternative over beef, but not when it's batter fried! One serving of chicken nuggets has the equivalent of five pats of butter, over twice of what you would get in a regular hamburger. And the fat it's soaked in is purely saturated, largely melted beef fat. A chicken sandwich is no health package either. This greasy sandwich has enough fat to equal 11 pats of butter, unless the chicken is grilled.

* Croissant Sandwiches aren't a whole lot more than "breakfast on a grease bun"! Most of the croissants have the equivalant of more than 4.5 pats of butter and the toppings add insult to injury!

*   Salad bars can be a good way to add fiber and nutrients to a meal, but it's only the salad vegetables that do so. The mayonnaise based salads, the croutons, and the bacon bits should be left on the bar, and dressing used sparingly. Use less dressing with extra lemon juice or vinegar for moistness.

*   Frozen yogurt, although lower in fat and cholesterol, contains more sugar than ice cream - so it is <u>not</u> a perfectly healthy substitute. This also applies to the frozen Tofu desserts. Look for some of the new sorbet-like frozen desserts that are primarily fruit. They will contain some sugar, but usually not in such high amounts.

Stop! Don't get discouraged and think you can't ever eat fast foods and still be healthy! You can have a healthy fast food meal, but you must learn to make good choices. The trick is to learn what you CAN eat and then think positively. Rather than feeling dismayed about everything you can't order, use your creativity and knowledge to find things you can.

The man who believes he can do something is probably right, and so is the man who believes he can't.

Here are our HEALTHY FAST FOOD CHOICES to help you:

BURGER KING
Hamburger Deluxe (no mayo!) - for women
Whopper (no mayo!) - for men
(A chicken sandwich has enough fat to equal 11 pats of butter!)
B.K. Broiler Chicken Sandwich (without dressing or mayo!)
Chunky Chicken Salad

MCDONALDS
Quarter pounder
Oriental Chicken Salad; crackers for complex carbohydrate

Chunky Chicken Salad (with your own whole grain, low salt crackers
for carbohydrate) and Lite Vinaigrette Dressing

Hamburger (small)
McLean Deluxe Sandwich (no mayo)
Chicken Fajitas

WENDY'S
Stuffed Potatoes - (plain without cheese sauce; get with chili insted)
Salad Bar - use raw vegetables as desired (avoid potato salad,
macaroni salad, and so forth; use garbanzo beans or chili for protein)
Single Hamburger on bun,without mayo
Caesar Side Salad (without dressing)
Grilled Chicken Sandwich

WENDY'S (continued)

Baked Potato (plain, without cheese sauce; get with chili instead)

Jr. Hamburger (without mayo)

HARDEE'S

Chicken 'n' Pasta Salad

Grilled Chicken Sandwich (no mayo!)

Hamburger (no mayo)

STEAK 'N SHAKE

Steakburger (no mayo!)

3-Way Chili

CHICK-FIL-A

Grilled Chicken Salad (no-oil salad dressing)

Grilled Chicken Sandwich (no mayo!)

TACO BELL

Soft Taco (chicken)

Taco, hardshell (chicken)

Fiesta Tostada

DAIRY QUEEN

BBQ Beef Sandwich

Grilled Chicken Fillet Sandwich (no sauce!)

ARBY'S OR RAX

Arby's Roast Beef or Chicken Sandwich (no mayo!)

Rax Turkey (no mayo!)

Roast Beef Sandwich (no sauce)

Arby's Fajita Pita

PIZZA PLACES

Personal-size cheese pizza, with vegetables if desired (eat three quarters and save the remaining quarter for a snack)

Thin crust 13″ (medium)cheese pizza with vegetables if desired (no sausage or pepperoni) 2 slices for women; 3 slices for men

SUB SHOPS OR DELI

Mini-sub (turkey, roast beef no oil or mayo)

Snack sub - 6 inches (turkey, roast beef cheese no oil or mayo)

Avoid Tuna subs - loaded with fat!

Deli and grocery stores will usually make you turkey, roast beef or Jarlsberg Lite sandwiches (ask for 3 ounces of meat on sandwich).

Menus
and
Recipes

PERFECT BREAKFASTS
THAT ARE QUICK, EASY AND DELICIOUS!

Remember — breakfast is the "stick" that stokes your metabolic fire. You need more than just a piece of toast and coffee to give your day a "Sunny Beginning." Try the following breakfast ideas, a different one every day, for a wonderful variety of ways to start your day just right!

1) **<u>CHEESE DANISH</u>**

1/2 whole wheat English muffin
2 Tbsp. Light Cream Cheese
2 Tbsp. raisins OR 1 Tbsp. all fruit preserves

Spread muffin with Light Cream Cheese; if possible, warm in toaster oven. Top with raisins or preserves. (Another marvelous choice: mash 1/4 cup fresh berries and put on top of cheese and muffin.) Makes 1 serving.

1 Complex CHO: Muffin / 1 oz. Protein: Cheese
1 Simple CHO: Raisins or Jam

2) <u>OATMEAL WITH A DIFFERENCE</u>

1/3 cup Old Fashioned Oats
3/4 cup skim milk
1/4 cup unsweetened apple juice

1 Tbsp. raisins
cinnamon
1/2 tsp. vanilla

Bring milk, apple juice and oatmeal to a boil. Gently cook for 5 minutes, stirring occasionally. Add raisins, vanilla and cinnamon; let sit covered for 2-3 minutes to thicken.
Makes 1 serving.

1 Complex CHO: Oats / 1 oz. Protein: Milk
1 Simple CHO: Juice and Raisins

3) <u>PEANUT BUTTER DANISH</u>

1 slice 100% whole grain bread
1 Tbsp. natural peanut butter

1/2 banana
6 oz. skim milk

Slice banana lengthwise and place with inside facing down on the slice of bread. Top with peanut butter. Broil until peanut butter is slightly brown and bubbly. Surprise! Have with an 6 oz. glass of skim milk.
Makes 1 serving.

1 Complex CHO: Bread / 1 oz. Protein: Peanut Butter and milk
1 Simple CHO: Banana

4) **SUNDAY FRENCH TOAST**

4 egg whites, lightly beaten
1 tsp. vanilla
1 cup skim milk
1/2 tsp. cinnamon
4 slices whole wheat bread
Fruit Preserves (no sugar) or mashed fresh fruit

You can freeze the extras and pop them in the microwave on a busy morning.

Beat together egg whites, milk, vanilla and cinnamon. Add bread slices one at a time, letting the bread absorb liquid in the process. May let sit for a few minutes. Spray non-stick skillet with cooking spray and heat. Gently lift the bread with spatula into skillet and cook until golden brown on each side. Serve topped with 1/2 cup fresh fruit or 1 Tbsp. preserves.
Makes 2 servings.

1 Complex CHO: Bread / 1 oz. Protein: Eggs, Milk
1 Simple CHO: Fruit

Add the juice of half an orange and it's even better!

5) **PERFECT BOWL OF CEREAL**

3/4 cup approved cereal
3/4 cup skim milk
1 Tbsp. unprocessed wheat bran AND 1 Tbsp. oat bran
1/2 cup fruit OR 1 small banana OR 2 Tbsp. raisins (1 tiny box)

APPROVED CEREALS: Kellogg's Nutrigrain (all types), Grapenuts (only use 1/4 cup, however), Shredded Wheat, Shredded Wheat-N-Bran, Puffed Wheat, Puffed Rice, oatmeal, Wheatena, Raisin Squares, Oat Bran, Muesli

1 Complex CHO: Cereal / 1 oz. Protein: Milk
1 Simple CHO: Fruit

6) **BREAKFAST SHAKE**

1/2 cup frozen fruit *   **2 Tbsp. non-fat dry milk**
1 cup skim milk   **2 Tbsp. wheat germ**
1 tsp. vanilla   **2 tsp. oat bran**

Blend frozen fruit in blender. Add remaining ingredients and continue blending till smooth.

1 Complex CHO: Wheat Germ and Bran / 2 oz. Protein: Milk
1 Simple CHO: Fruit

*Don't throw away your very ripe bananas. Peel and freeze in freezer bags and use for your shakes.

118

7) **BREAKFAST PARFAIT**

1/2 cup plain, nonfat yogurt
1/2 cup blueberries OR 1 small mashed banana OR 1/2 cup unsweetened crushed pineapple
     (strawberries are too tart)
1/4 cup Grapenuts
1 Tbsp. all fruit jam
cinnamon

Layer parfait style into tall parfait glass yogurt, fruit and cereal. Sprinkle with cinnamon and ENJOY!

1 Complex CHO: Cereal / 1 oz. Protein: Yogurt
1 Simple CHO: Fruit

8) **CHEESE APPLE SURPRISE**

1 slice whole wheat bread	**1/2 apple, thinly sliced**
1 Tbsp. raisins	**1 oz. mozzarella cheese**

Top bread with apple and raisins. Place cheese on apple-raisin layer. Broil until cheese is bubbly.
Makes 1 serving.

1 Complex CHO: Bread / 1 oz. Protein: Cheese
1 Simple CHO: Apple and Raisins

9) **MUFFIN MAGIC**

Oat Bran Muffin (your complex carbohydrate) - page 120
8 oz. Skim Milk or Plain, Nonfat Yogurt (your protein)
Fresh Fruit (your simple carbohydrate)

OAT BRAN MUFFINS

2-1/4 cups oat bran
1/4 cup honey
1-1/4 cups skim milk
2 egg whites
2 Tbsp. Puritan or Safflower oil
1 Tbsp. baking powder
3/4 tsp. cinnamon
1/2 tsp. pumpkin or apple pie spice
1/4 tsp salt
1/4 cup raisins

Preheat the oven to 425 degrees. Process the oat bran with large blade in food processor while mixing other ingredients (this will "lighten up" the muffins). Mix the milk, egg whites, honey and oil together. Add the baking powder, spices and salt to the bran in processor; blend. Add the liquid mixture and process just until blended. Add raisins.

Line muffin pans with paper baking cups, and fill with batter. Bake 15 to 17 minutes; test for doneness at 15 minutes with a toothpick — it should come out moist but not wet. Makes 12 muffins. Store in a plastic bag to retain moisture. If you will not use these in three days, store in freezer and thaw one at a time.

Optional: Omit pie spice, 1/2 cup skim milk and raisins. Add 1 small can crushed pineapple and 1 small mashed banana.

WONDERFUL LUNCHES

Don't skip lunch, and don't get into a rut either! For a lunch that will refresh you and keep your energy high, try one of these delicious and fast complete meals.

1) <u>SEAFOOD SALAD</u>

3/4 cup waterpacked tuna or salmon
1 tsp. Dijon mustard
1 Tbsp. reduced calorie mayonnaise
pepper to taste

1 stalk chopped celery
1/4 tsp. beau monde   (optional)
1/4 tsp. dill
8 seasoned Ry-Krisp

Mix together ingredients. Serve on bed of torn romaine lettuce with Ry-Krisp and fresh fruit.

Complex CHO: Crackers / Protein: Fish
Simple CHO: Fruit / Added Fat: Mayonnaise

2) <u>PEANUT BUTTER AND BANANA SANDWICH</u>

1 Tbsp. natural peanut butter (never, never commercial)
2 slices of whole wheat bread
1 small sliced banana
6 oz. skim milk

Make sandwich with bread, peanut butter and sliced banana.
Have with 6 oz. skim milk.

Complex CHO: Bread / Protein: Peanut Butter and Skim Milk
Simple CHO: Banana

121

3) <u>CHEF'S SALAD</u>

As many sliced veggies as possible (try to have at least 5)
Romaine lettuce
2 oz. chicken, turkey or low-fat cheese

Toss vegetables with lettuce; top with meat or cheese. You may use croutons made by toasting 2 pieces whole wheat that have been sprinkled with garlic powder (not salt!) Cut these into cubes and store in jar or tin to have on hand. Serve with whole grain crackers and fresh fruit.

Complex CHO: Crackers and Croutons / Protein: Turkey
Simple CHO: Fruit / Added Fat: 1 Tbsp. Dressing

4) <u>CHICKEN, TURKEY OR ROAST BEEF SANDWICH</u>

2 oz. meat (trimmed of all fat)
2 slices whole wheat bread
1 tsp. mayonnaise and/or mustard
lettuce and sliced tomato

Spread bread with mayo and/or mustard. Layer with meat of choice; top with lettuce and tomato. Serve with a delicious piece of fruit.

Complex CHO: Bread / Protein: Turkey
Simple CHO: Fruit / Added Fat: Mayonnaise

5) **CHICKEN OF THE LAND OR SEA APPLE SANDWICH**

1/2 cup waterpacked tuna or chicken
1 small stalk of chopped celery
1 Tbsp. reduced calorie mayonnaise

1 small chopped apple
1 whole wheat pita
romaine lettuce leaves

Mix together first 4 ingredients. Stuff into 2 halved pita lined with lettuce.

Complex CHO: Pita / Protein: Chicken
Simple CHO: Fruit / Added Fat: Mayonnaise

6) **VEGGIE SANDWICH**

1 whole wheat pita
2 oz. cheese (mozzarella, skimmed cheddar, or Lorraine Swiss)
a few mushrooms and green pepper rings
sliced tomato

Stuff halved pita with 1 oz. cheese each and vegetables. Microwave on high for 2 to 3 minutes. Add a couple of tomato slices and be ready for a treat. Serve with a fruit juice spritzer (1/2 cup juice mixed with club soda or seltzer) over ice.

Complex CHO: Pita / Protein: Cheese
Simple CHO: Juice

123

7) <u>HEALTHY HAMBURGER</u>

1 whole wheat hamburger bun
3 oz. uncooked ground round or ground turkey patty
lettuce and tomato slices

Grill or broil hamburger patty (the fat will drain through rack and will cook meat down to 2 to 2-1/2 oz.) Place on whole wheat bun with lettuce, tomato slices, mustard and a small amount of ketchup (if desired). 1 pound of ground round = five 2 oz. patties after cooking. Serve with Melon Slices.

Complex CHO: Bun / Protein: Hamburger
Simple CHO: Melon

8) <u>CARROT-CHEESE MELT</u>

2 coarsely grated carrots (about 1/2 cup)
2 slices whole wheat bread
1-1/2 oz. grated mozzarella cheese

Mix together carrots and cheese. Spread bread with carrot-cheese mix. Grill in teflon skillet till cheese melts. Add tomato slices, lettuce (and even alfalfa sprouts!).

Complex CHO: Bread / Protein: Cheese
Simple CHO: Carrots

EASY, DELICIOUS AND HEALTHY DINNERS

There are times that having a basic format to work from can be invaluable! These are eight meals that you can use as a beginning place: they are perfectly balanced, everyone will like them, and they are easy! Freeze properly portioned leftovers in freezer Zip Lock® bags for quick meals when you need them most!

1) **OVEN BAKED CHICKEN** — (your protein)
   PEAS ROSEMARY — (your complex carbohydrate and meal's fat)
   STEAMED CABBAGE — (your simple carbohydrate)
   CARROT-RAISIN SALAD — (the rest of your simple carbohydrate)

<u>OVEN BAKED CHICKEN</u> *It tastes like fried chicken!*

2 egg whites, lightly beaten	**1 Tbsp. water**
2 cups Nutrigrain Wheat cereal, crushed	**1/4 tsp. garlic powder**
1/4 tsp. pepper	**1/4 tsp. seasoned salt (optional)**
6 chicken half-breasts, deboned and skinned	

Mix together egg and water in shallow dish; set aside. Combine crushed cereal and spices. Dip chicken in egg mixture, then dredge in cereal mixture, coating well. Arrange in baking pan coated with cooking spray. Bake, uncovered, at 350 degrees for 45 minutes, or until tender. Yields 6 servings each, giving you your protein and part of your complex carbohydrate.

125

PEAS ROSEMARY

1 pkg. frozen peas, cooked and drained
2 tsp. olive oil
2 cloves minced garlic
1/4 cup chopped onion

1/4 tsp. pepper
1 tsp. rosemary
1/4 tsp. salt (optional)

Saute garlic and onion in oil till tender. Add rosemary, salt and pepper and continue to saute one more minute. Toss with peas. Makes 4 servings; one serving would be your complex carbohydrate.

CARROT SALAD A LA DIFFERENCE

1 lb. coarsely grated carrots
2 medium apples, grated
1 cup firm plain, nonfat yogurt
1/2 cup crushed unsweetened pineapple
1/2 cup raisins

Combine all ingredients and chill. Makes 12 servings; 1 cup serving counts as your simple carbohydrate.

2) **MARVELOUS MEATLOAF** — (your protein and part of your complex carbohydrates)
   CORN ON COB — (your complex carbohydrate)
   COLORFUL GREEN BEANS — (your simple carbohydrate)
   ROMAINE SALAD — (your healthy munchie)

MARVELOUS MEATLOAF

2 lbs. ground round or ground turkey
2 cups old fashioned oats
1 Tbsp. worcestershire sauce
1 tsp. dry mustard
1/4 cup skim milk
3/4 cup tomato sauce

1/2 tsp. each salt and pepper
3/4 cup minced onion
1/4 green pepper, minced
2 eggs, slightly beaten

In large bowl, mix together all ingredients except for 1/2 cup of the tomato sauce. Shape meat into 2 loaves and place in loaf pans sprayed with cooking spray. Spread the additional 1/2 cup tomato sauce on top. Bake in 400 degree oven for 40 minutes. A 3 oz. serving counts as your protein.

COLORFUL GREEN BEANS

1 lb. green beans
1/2 cup chopped onion
1/2 tsp. salt (optional)
2 medium tomatoes, peeled and cut into 8 wedges

1 tsp. olive oil
1/2 cup chopped celery
1/4 tsp. pepper

Remove strings from beans; wash and cut diagonally into 2" pieces. Heat oil in skillet, add onion and celery to skillet and saute until tender; add beans, salt and pepper. Cover and simmer 10 minutes, stirring occasionally. Add tomato; cover and cook an additional 5 minutes. Makes 4 servings; each serving counts as your simple carbohydrate.

3) **HAWAIIAN CHICKEN** — (your protein)
   WILD RICE PILAF — (your complex carbohydrate)
   GREEN BEANS AND MUSHROOMS — (your simple carbohydrate)
   SLICED TOMATOES — (your healthy munchie)

HAWAIIAN CHICKEN

1/3 cup unsweetened pineapple juice   **2 cloves garlic**
1/3 cup low sodium soy sauce   **1 Tbsp. parsley**
1/3 cup sherry or alcohol-free Chardonnay   **ground pepper to taste**
4 skinned chicken breasts

Mix all but chicken. Marinate chicken breasts (skinned, deboned and split lengthwise) for 3-4 hours or overnight. (The marinade adds no significant calories.) Grill. Makes 4 servings; one serving would be your protein.

WILD RICE PILAF

1 tsp. olive oil
1 medium onion, chopped
1 clove minced garlic
1 stalk celery, chopped
2-1/3 cups chicken broth

1/4 cup wild rice
3/4 cup brown rice
1/4 tsp. salt (optional)
1 Tbsp. parsley

Saute vegetables in medium saucepan with 1 tsp. olive oil. Add broth and optional salt; bring to boil and add rices. Boil for one minute - reduce heat and simmer for 45 minutes until the liquid is absorbed. Garnish with parsley. Makes 6 half-cup servings; 1 cup would be your complex carbohydrate.

GREEN BEANS WITH MUSHROOMS

1 tsp. olive oil
1 clove minced garlic
1/2 lb. washed mushrooms
1/2 tsp. rosemary
1/2 tsp. basil

1 Tbsp. parsley
1/2 tsp. salt (optional)
1/4 tsp. pepper
1 lb. steamed green beans

Saute garlic and mushrooms in olive oil in non-stick pan for 3–4 minutes. Add spices and simmer covered for another minute. Toss well with beans. Makes 4 servings; each counts as your simple carbohydrate.

129

4) **SALMON OF THE DAY** — (this is your protein)
   BAKED SWEET POTATO — (this is your complex carbohydrate)
   STEAMED BROCCOLI — (this is your simple carbohydrate)
   WALDORF SALAD — (this is your simple carbohydrate)

BAKED SALMON IN A POUCH

1/4 cup cider vinegar
1/2 tsp. Dijon mustard
1/2 tsp. dillweed
1/4 tsp. minced garlic

4 salmon steaks, 1" thick (approx. 1 lb.)
1 sliced green pepper
1 thinly sliced tomato
1 minced scallion

Combine vinegar, mustard, dill and garlic in glass baking dish. Add salmon and marinate for 10 minutes. Turn salmon over and marinate 10 minutes more. Cut four 8" x 8" sheets of aluminum foil. For each serving, place a salmon steak in the center of foil. Distribute peppers, tomatoes and scallions on top. Drizzle with marinade. Fold and pinch foil to seal fish inside. Bake at 375 degrees for 15 to 20 minutes. Remove from foil and serve immediately. Makes 4 servings; each gives you protein.

Love is like the 5 loaves and 2 fishes. It doesn't start to multiply until you share it.

POACHED SALMON

1-1/2 cups Chablis or other white wine
1 lemon, sliced
1 tsp. dried dillweed
1/4 tsp. pepper
4 salmon steaks, 1" thick (approx. 1 lb.)

1/2 cup water
1 onion, sliced
4 sprigs parsley
extra sliced lemon

Combine all ingredients except fish and additional lemon slices in a large skillet. Bring to a boil; cover, reduce heat, and simmer 5 minutes. Add salmon steaks or fillets; cover and simmer 8 minutes or until fish flakes easily. Remove from skillet; garnish with lemon slices. Makes 4 servings; each gives you protein.

GRILLED SALMON

1/2 tsp. allspice
1 tsp. cardamon (optional)
2 cloves garlic, minced

1/3 cup lime juice
1-1/3 lbs. salmon steaks, about 1" thick
additional lime slices

Combine spices with garlic and lime juice. Arrange salmon in a single layer in shallow dish; cover with marinade. Let stand for 15 minutes, then turn over and let stand for 15 minutes more. Grill salmon for 5 minutes per side or until it flakes easily. Makes 4 servings; 1 serving counts as protein.

131

SALMON LOAF

1 medium onion, chopped
3/4 cup old fashioned oats (uncooked)
1/2 cup unprocessed bran
15-1/2 oz. can salmon, drained
1 cup buttermilk
1/4 tsp. garlic powder

2 eggs, lightly beaten
1 Tbsp. parsley
1/2 tsp. dill
1/2 tsp. salt, if desired
1/4 tsp. pepper
lemon and parsley to garnish

Mix together all ingredients. Pack into an 8-1/2 x 4-1/2 inch bread pan sprayed with non-stick spray. Bake at 350 degrees for 40 minutes, until firm. Garnish with lemon wedges and parsley. Makes 6 servings; each serving counts as your protein and part of your complex carbohydrate.

WALDORF IN DISGUISE

2 large apples, in chunks
1/2 cup unsweetened pineapple chunks
1/2 stalk chopped celery
1/2 cup sliced carrot
1 sliced green pepper

1 small orange, sectioned
1/4 cup raisins
1-1/4 cups Orange Yogurt dressing
2 Tbsp. chopped walnuts

Combine apples, pineapple, celery, carrots, green pepper, orange and raisins. Add dressing, mixing well. Chill. Sprinkle with chopped nuts before serving. Makes 6 half-cup servings, each giving 2 servings of simple carbohydrates.

132

Dressing:

3/4 cup plain low-fat yogurt
juice from 1/2 lemon

1/2 cup orange juice
dash salt and cinnamon

*Mix a lot of dressing at one time and keep in refrigerator for a wonderful fruit topping

5) **CHILI CON CARNE** — (this is your protein, complex and simple carbohydrate)
   ROMAINE SALAD — (this is your healthy munchie)
   SLICED MELON — (this is more simple carbohydrate)

CHILI CON CARNE*

1 lb. ground round or ground turkey
2 tsp. olive oil
1 cup chopped onion
2 cloves crushed garlic
1 cup chopped celery
3 cups green peppers, chopped
1 15-1/2 oz. can tomato sauce

1 28 oz. can undrained tomatoes
1 tsp. basil
2-3 tsp. chili powder
1 tsp. salt (optional)
1/8 tsp. pepper
1 medium can red kidney beans,
**   drained and rinsed**

Place ground meat in hard plastic colander; place colander
in glass bowl in microwave. Microwave on high for 3 minutes; break up.
Continue cooking another 3 minutes, or until brown; stir again. In a 3-4
qt. sauce pan, heat oil and add 3/4 cup of the onions, the garlic, the celery, and 1 cup of
the green peppers. Saute 5-8 minutes over moderate heat, stirring occasionally, until

tender. Add tomatoes, breaking them up as you stir them in. Stir
in the browned meat, chili powder, basil, salt and pepper. Cover
and simmer 1 hour over low heat. Uncover and simmer 40-60 minutes
longer, stirring occasionally to develop flavor. Stir in the
beans and cook 5 minutes longer. Garnish with remaining onions
and green peppers to make it pretty. 2 cups = 1 serving.
*May make this vegetarian by adding another can of kidney beans
and serving over rice or pasta.

6) **CHICKEN OF THE DAY** — (your protein and your complex CHO)
   STEAMED ASPARAGUS — (counts as part of your simple CHO)
   SPINACH AND APPLE SALAD — (counts as health munchie and
   the meal's added fat)

BASQUE CHICKEN

1 lg. green pepper, in strips
2 med. onions, sliced and in rings
1/4 lb. thinly sliced mushrooms
2 cloves minced garlic
8 red potatoes, thinly sliced
2 chicken breasts, skinned
  deboned and split lengthwise

1/2 tsp. salt (optional)
1/4 tsp. black pepper
1/4 tsp. cayenne
1-1/2 cups tomato puree
1/4 cup dry white wine
2 tsp. cornstarch
1 tbsp. water

Place vegetables in roasting pan. Place chicken pieces over
vegetables; sprinkle with spices. Mix tomato puree and wine; pour
into roasting pan. Bake at 375 degrees for 1 hour uncovered or

134

until tender and browned. Pour cooking liquid with vegetables into skillet. Mix cornstarch and water; stir into skillet. Heat to boiling; cook, stirring constantly until thickened and clear. Pour sauce and vegetables over chicken and serve. This makes 4 servings; 1 piece of chicken counts as your protein, two potatoes count as your complex carbohydrate, and 1 cup sauce counts as your simple carbohydrate.

STIR FRY CHICKEN WITH SNOW PEAS

2 cloves garlic, minced
2 Tbsp. low sodium soy sauce
1 Tbsp. sherry
2 Tbsp. cornstarch
2 split chicken breasts, cut into 1 inch cubes

20 snow pea pods, sliced
1/2 cup water chestnut, drained
1/2 cup chicken stock
2 tsp. peanut or canola oil

Mix together garlic, soy sauce, sherry, and cornstarch; marinate chicken pieces in mixture for 15 minutes. Spray wok with non-stick cooking spray, then heat with 2 tsp. peanut oil. Add chicken; stir fry for 30 seconds. Add chicken broth; stir fry until thickened. Serve immediately. Wonderful over brown rice. Makes 2 servings; each gives 2-3 oz. protein, 1 simple carbohydrate and 1 added fat. The brown rice would be your complex carbohydrate.

Doing nothing is tiresome - you can't stop and rest.

135

SPINACH AND APPLE SALAD

1 Tbsp. canola oil
1-1/2 tsp. basil
1 tsp. onion powder
1/2 tsp. salt (optional)
1/8 tsp. pepper

3/4 cup apple juice
2 Tbsp. cider vinegar
4 cups spinach, torn in pieces
2 cups thinly sliced apple
1/2 cup orange segments (optional)

Prepare dressing: In small bowl, combine oil, basil, onion powder, salt and pepper; set aside 10 minutes for flavors to blend. Stir in apple juice and vinegar. In large bowl, combine spinach, apple and oranges. Toss with 1/2 cup dressing; serve immediately. Refrigerate remaining dressing for other salads or marinade. Makes 6 healthy munchie servings and 1 added fat/svg.

7) **ITALIAN SWISS STEAK** — (your protein)
    WHOLE WHEAT NOODLES — (your complex carbohydrate)
    STEAMED YELLOW SQUASH — (part of your simple carbohydrate)
    ROMAINE LETTUCE SALAD — (your healthy munchie)

ITALIAN SWISS STEAK

1 lb. lean round steak*, trimmed of fat
1/2 cup water
1 medium onion, thinly sliced
1 green pepper, thinly sliced
2 small tomatoes, cut in wedges
1/4 lb. mushrooms

1/2 tsp. basil
1/2 tsp. oregano
1 Tbsp. parsley
1/2 tsp. garlic powder
1/4 tsp. each salt and pepper

Brown steak in non-stick skillet; add water. Place in roasting pan with cover. Top with vegetables and water; sprinkle with spices. Cover and bake at 350 degrees for 1-1/2 hours. Serve over whole wheat noodles. Makes 4 servings; one serving counts as your protein and part of your simple carbohydrate.

*May use 2 large chicken breasts, deboned, skinned and split

8) **EASY CHICKEN AND RICE** — (your protein, your complex carbohydrate and part of your simple carbohydrate)

    CAESAR SALAD — (your healthy munchie and added fat)
      OR
    PEACH PIZZAZZ — (this would be more simple carbohydrate)

EASY CHICKEN AND RICE — A great one dish meal

2 cups chicken stock, or low sodium chicken bouillon

3/4 cup water	**1/2 tsp. salt (optional)**
1 cup brown rice, uncooked	**1/4 tsp. black pepper**
4 boneless chicken breasts, skinned	**1/2 tsp. garlic powder**
1 small onion, chopped	**1/2 tsp. rosemary**
1 Tbsp. dried parsley	**1 tsp. dried tarragon**

1 bag (16 oz.) frozen cuts of vegetables (i.e. California Mix)

Pour chicken stock and water into a large roasting pan. Add brown rice and top with chicken breasts. Sprinkle with chopped onion, herbs and spices. Cover pan with lid. Bake for 1-1/2 hours, adding the frozen vegetables during the last 30 minutes of cooking. This is a classic meal-in-one: 1 serving give 3 oz. protein, 2 complex carbohydrates and 1 simple carbohydrate.

CAESAR SALAD

4 cups washed, torn romaine
1 clove minced garlic
1-1/2 Tbsp. olive oil
1/2 tsp. dry mustard
1 tsp. worcestershire sauce
1/8 tsp. coarse black pepper

1/8 tsp. salt (optional)
1 coddled egg*
juice of 1 lemon
1/4 cup grated parmesan
Croutons made from 2 slices whole wheat
    bread sprinkled with garlic powder,
    toasted till brown

Rub bottom and sides of large salad bowl with garlic; leave in bowl. Add oil, mustard, worcestershire sauce and spices; beat together with fork. Add chilled romaine lettuce; toss well. Top with coddled egg and lemon juice; toss till lettuce is well covered. Top with parmesan and croutons. Toss well and enjoy! Makes 6 servings. This gives a healthy munchie and an added fat.

*Coddle an egg by immersing the egg in shell in boiling water 30 seconds.

PEACH PIZZAZZ

4 peach halves, fresh or packed in own juice, without sugar
3 Tbsp. fat-free cream cheese
cinnamon

Place peach halves on lettuce leaves; top with 2 tsp. cheese and sprinkle with cinnamon. Makes 4 servings; each counts as simple carbohydrate.

138

9) **SPAGHETTI PIE** — (your protein, complex carbohydrate and part of your simple carbohydrate)
   MARINATED VEGGIES — (variety of raw veggies marinated in No-Oil Italian Dressing, sprinkled with Parmesan Cheese)

SPAGHETTI PIE

6 oz. Vermicelli or whole wheat pasta	**8 oz. can stewed tomatoes**
2 tsp. olive oil	**6 oz. can tomato paste**
1/3 cup grated Parmesan Cheese	**3/4 tsp. dried oregano**
2 egg whites, well beaten	**1/4 tsp. salt (optional)**
1/2 lb. ground turkey*	**1/2 tsp. garlic powder**
1/2 cup chopped onion	**1 cup part skimmed Ricotta Cheese**
1/4 cup chopped green pepper	**1/2 cup shredded Mozzarella Cheese**

Cook pasta according to package directions; drain. Stir olive oil and Parmesan Cheese into hot pasta. Add egg whites, stirring well. Spoon mixture into a 10" pie plate. Use a spoon to shape the spaghetti into a pie shell. Microwave at HIGH uncovered 3 minutes or until set. Set aside.

Crumble turkey in a colander, stir in onion and green pepper. Cover with plastic wrap and microwave at HIGH 5-6 minutes, stirring every 2 minutes. Let drain well. Put into a bowl and stir in tomatoes, tomato paste and seasonings. Cover and microwave at HIGH 3-1/2 to 4 minutes, stirring once. Set aside.

Spread Ricotta evenly over pie shell. Top with meat sauce. Cover with plastic wrap and microwave at HIGH 6 to 6-1/2 minutes; sprinkle with Mozzarella Cheese. Microwave uncovered at HIGH 30 seconds, or until cheese begins to melt.

6 servings = 2 oz. protein, 1 complex and 1 simple carbohydrate.

*May substitute ground round; drain **well** after cooking.

SURVIVAL PLANNING FOR QUICK MEALS

(This is for the people with the philosophy that
"If it takes longer to cook it than to eat it, FORGET IT!")

There are few people these days with the time or inclination to spend all afternoon preparing the dinner meal each day. Spending just an hour on a weekend to put together some of the basics will allow each night's meal to be a healthy delight with a minimum of effort.

BASIC GAME PLAN: (Do once a week)

1) Prepare the marinade for Hawaiian Chicken; marinate enough boneless chicken breasts for 2 meals: 1/2 can be sliced and used in stir-fry with vegetables one night - the other breasts can be put on the grill.

2) Cook a big pot of brown rice - it can be heated during the week as needed. Or measure it out in servings, freeze in Zip Lock® bags and reheat in microwave or boiling water.

3) Cook a big pot of whole wheat pasta for quick heat-ups during the week.

The more you prepare
The luckier you get!

140

4) Make a pot of tomato sauce - it can be tossed with pasta, used to make "pita pizza," used to make lasagna, or as topping for meats. You may also keep commercial sauce made without salt or sugar for extra ease.

5) Cook a pot of pinto beans: they can be used one night as beans and rice, another night pureed and used on warm tortillas with shredded lettuce, chopped tomatoes and picante sauce as bean burritos.

6) Cut up a plastic bag full of various vegetables: zucchini, broccoli, cauliflower, mushrooms, carrots, etc. Part may be marinated in low calorie Italian dressing for a quick salad - remaining may be used to steam or stir-fry.

7) For "extra quick" stir-fry - use frozen bags of assorted vegetable mixes. The vegetables are already cut and they can be fully cooked in 4 minutes! Bags of frozen peas can also be used for a quick complex carbohydrate.

8) A basic salad is torn romaine lettuce topped with a tomato, a no-oil Italian dressing and a sprinkle of parmesan.

9) Sliced melon or fresh strawberries are a refreshing and quick complement to any meal!

A WEEK OF FAST AND FABULOUS DINNERS

Monday: Grilled Marinated Chicken Breast
Brown Rice
Steamed Vegetables
Romaine Lettuce Salad

Tuesday: Whole Wheat Pasta Topped with Tomato Sauce
and Parmesan Cheese
Steamed Broccoli
Marinated Vegetables
Fresh Fruit Medley Topped with Yogurt

Wednesday: Stir-fried Vegetables and Chicken Tossed with Pasta
Romaine Lettuce Salad

Thursday: Beans over Brown Rice
Steamed Vegetables
Fresh Fruit

Friday: Grilled Chicken on Whole Wheat Bun
Lettuce and Tomato Slices
Marinated Vegetable Salad

Saturday: GO OUT TO EAT (or use up any leftovers)

Sunday: Bean Burritos
Sliced Melon

Holidays and Parties That Celebrate Life

HOLIDAYS AND PARTIES THAT CELEBRATE LIFE!

Here are survival tips for remaining alive, well and merry in a world that overeats: HAPPY HOLIDAYS!

1.   Always eat a healthy snack before going to parties so that your "appetite for the appetizers" will be in control!

2.   Don't try to starve the day of a big party! You will only slow down your metabolism and set yourself up for a gorge because you will be so hungry. Instead, eat smaller, evenly spaced meals throughout the day.

3.   Remember that it's not the "big parties" that are a problem but the day by day eating. Eating well in between the "big days" will help to stabilize your body. Avoid the "I've blown it now" syndrome and let each day be a new beginning.

4.   Try to make the focus of parties more than just the food itself. Plan other activities besides eating! Games are fun for everyone and give a new direction from the usual gorge. Talk to friends in rooms other than where the food is served.

5.   Never tell people you are dieting; it is self sabotage! You will instantly be a candidate to be talked (or badgered!) into everything. If you feel you must say anything, just say "I am not hungry quite yet." Don't look pitiful in a corner! No one ever notices that the life of the party isn't eating.

RECIPES FOR WONDERFULLY HEALTHY HOLIDAYS

BEST BARBECUE

Date-Cheese Ball   Raw Vegetable Platter with Dips

Hawaiian Chicken*

Corn on the Cob   Cole Slaw with a Difference

Watermelon Quarters   Date Bars

DATE-CHEESE BALL

2 8 oz. pkgs. fat-free cream cheese
2 Tbsp. (or more) low-fat milk
1/2 cup chopped walnuts

8 oz. chopped dates
(not sugar-coated)

Process in food processor or blender until evenly mixed. Use milk to help blend more easily. Shape into ball - garnish with grapes and walnuts. Best served with Norwegian Flat Breads. 2 Tbsp. = 1 protein and 1 simple carbohydrate.

ZESTY DIP

8 oz. low-fat cottage cheese
1 Tbsp. lemon juice
2 tsp. celery seeds
1 tsp. worcestershire sauce

1/2 tsp. garlic powder
1/8 tsp. onion powder
1/4 tsp. salt (optional)
dash red pepper sauce

Combine all ingredients in blender or processor. Process until cheese is consistency of sour cream. Serve with fresh vegetables for dipping. 1/4 cup gives 1 oz. protein.

*See Index

145

HERB AND GARLIC DIP

1 cup low-fat cottage cheese
1/2 cup skim milk
2 Tbsp. fresh or 1 Tbsp. dried parsley
1 small red cabbage

1/8 tsp. curry powder
1/8 tsp. paprika
1 garlic clove
1/2 tsp. basil

Place cottage cheese, milk, spices and garlic in blender or food processor, process until smooth. Hollow out the head of cabbage from the top. Cut a slice from the stem end so the cabbage will rest firmly on its base. Spoon dip into cabbage. 1/4 cup gives 1 oz. protein

COLE SLAW WITH A DIFFERENCE

1/4 head of red cabbage
1/4 head of green cabbage
2 large carrots

8 oz. crushed unsweetened pineapple
1/2 cup plain nonfat yogurt
1/2 cup raisins

Grate cabbage and carrots in food processor or by hand. Mix rest of ingredients together. This may be made far in advance — the flavors blend together. Makes 8 servings each equaling 1 simple carbohydrate.

DATE BARS

1 cup whole wheat pastry flour
1/2 cup wheat germ
1 tsp. baking powder
2 tsp. cinnamon
1/4 tsp. ground allspice

1 cup dates, chopped
1/2 cup chopped walnuts
3 eggs, beaten
1/3 cup honey
1 tsp. vanilla extract

Combine the flour, wheat germ, baking powder, cinnamon, allspice, dates and walnuts in a medium mixing bowl. Mix the eggs, honey and vanilla together in a medium bowl, then fold into the dry ingredients. Spread the batter in a lightly oiled 9 x 13 inch baking pan. Bake at 350 degrees for about 20 minutes, until golden brown. Makes 24 bars, 2 bars equals 1 complex and 1 simple carbohydrate and 1 added fat.

The best way to keep children home is to make the home atmosphere pleasant - and let the air out of the tires.

HOLIDAY DINNER

Cranberry Salad Mold
Roast Turkey or Rosemary Roast Lamb
Wild Rice Pilaf* **Healthy Gravy**
Sweet Potatoes Glorious **Green Beans with Mushrooms***
Apple-Date Muffins **Fresh Fruit Pie**

CRANBERRY SALAD MOLD

2 envelopes unflavored gelatin
1 cup orange juice
1 - 6 oz. can apple juice concentrate
2 tbsp. honey
1 cup water

1 - 12 oz. bag cranberries
1 cup shredded carrot
1/2 cup raisins
1 cup chopped apple
1 cup diced celery

Sprinkle gelatin over juices and honey in small bowl, let soften 5 minutes. Meanwhile, combine cranberries and water in large saucepan. Bring to boiling. Lower heat and simmer 5 minutes. Add gelatin-juice mixture to cranberries. Stir until gelatin is dissolved, about 2 minutes. Let cool in refrigerator until thickened to consistency of egg whites. Add celery, carrot, raisins and apple; gently mix. Pour into a 6-cup mold that has been sprayed with non-stick cooking spray. Refrigerate overnight or until salad is firm. Makes 12 servings each counting as 2 simple carbohydrates.

*See index

148

ROAST TURKEY

Before roasting, slide a thin layer of celery leaves and thin slices of onion between skin and breast meat of turkey - it adds a rich flavor to the meat and the vegetables absorb much of the fat from the skin. Roast the turkey as you usually would.

TURKEY GRAVY — THE HEALTHY WAY

2 Tbsp. canola oil
1 Tbsp. cornstarch
1 bay leaf
1/4 cup white wine

1 clove minced garlic
1-1/2 cups heated chicken/turkey stock
(may use low sodium bouillon)

Heat oil in saucepan. Add garlic and cook about 30 seconds. Stir in cornstarch until smooth. Add stock, bay leaf and wine. Cook until sauce thickens, about 5 minutes. Remove bay leaf. Serve with turkey. Makes about 2 cups. Each 1/3 cup serving equals 1 added fat.

ROSEMARY ROAST LAMB

6-7 lbs. oven-ready leg of lamb, trimmed of all visible fat
2 sliced garlic cloves
1 tsp. olive oil
1 lb. Idaho potatoes in 1" chunks
1 cup chicken broth
1/2 tsp. garlic powder
1 lb. can tomatoes, drained

1 lb. eggplant, halved crosswise and cut into 1" spears
2 tsp. rosemary
1/2 tsp. each salt and pepper
1 lb. green beans boiled 5 minutes and drained
2-1/2 cups sliced onions

Heat oven to 400 degrees. With sharp knife make 6 small incisions in thickest part of meat and insert garlic slices. Rub meat with olive oil; sprinkle with rosemary and 1/2 tsp. each salt and pepper; press seasonings into meat. Put meat in large roasting pan and roast 1 hour and 15 minutes. Surround meat with vegetables, making two piles of each. Pour chicken broth over vegetables, making two piles of each. Pour chicken broth over vegetables and sprinkle with garlic powder, onions and tomatoes. Cover the pan with aluminum foil and bake 1 hour and 10 minutes more. Meat will be medium-rare to medium and internal temperature will register 150 degrees on a meat thermometer. Arrange sliced meat on platter surrounded with vegetables. 8 servings; each gives 3 oz. protein, 1 complex carbohydrate and 1 simple carbohydrate.

SWEET POTATOES GLORIOUS

4 lbs. sweet potatoes, boiled and peeled
2 Tbsp. cornstarch
1/2 tsp. salt (optional)
1-1/3 cups pineapple juice
1 small can crushed unsweetened pineapple

2 Tbsp. dry milk
3 eggs
1/2 tsp. cinnamon
2 tsp. nutmeg

Mash potatoes. Add all but pineapple — beat. Add pineapple and pour into casserole dish. Sprinkle with shredded coconut and walnuts as garnish. Bake at 350 degrees for 30 minutes. Freezes beautifully. 1/3 cup equals 1 complex carbohydrate.

God sends food for the birds but He doesn't throw it in the nest.

151

APPLE DATE MUFFINS - Delicious!

1-1/2 cups Shredded Wheat-N-Bran cereal	1/4 cup honey
1-1/2 cups whole wheat pastry flour	1 cup skim milk
1 Tbsp. baking powder	2 eggs
1/2 tsp. salt (optional)	1/2 cup walnuts
1/2 tsp. each cinnamon and apple pie spice	1 cup dates, chopped
2 Tbsp. Canola oil	3 cups chopped apples

Finely process cereal in blender or food processor. Mix with remaining dry ingredients; set aside. In another bowl, beat oil, honey and eggs until well blended. Add skim milk. Stir in flour mixture till well blended; fold in dates and nuts. Spray muffin tin with non-stick cooking spray or line with papers; fill 2/3 full. Sprinkle top with dash of cinnamon. Bake at 350 degrees for 25 minutes or until toothpick inserted in center comes out clean. Cool on wire rack for 10 minutes; remove from pan and cool completely. Makes 16 muffins each, giving a complex CHO, 1 simple CHO and 1 added fat.

FRESH FRUIT PIE

1 cup unsweetened* flaked coconut
2 egg whites, lightly beaten

Toss together and pat into pie pan. Bake at 325 degrees for 10 minutes; cool.

Layer into cooled pie shell:
2 bananas, sliced in orange juice and drained
1 pt. fresh sliced strawberries (or substitute sliced Kiwi)
15-1/2 oz. can of crushed unsweetened pineapple, cooked with 1 Tbsp. corn-starch to thicken

Sprinkle with more coconut and strawberries to garnish. Makes 8 servings, each equals 1 simple carbohydrate and 1 added fat.

*Available from natural food store

We always have time for the things we put first.

153

RECIPE INDEX AND NUTRITIONAL PROFILE

APPLE DATE MUFFINS, Page 152
Calories: 157; carbohydrate: 27 gm; protein: 4 gm; fat: 2 gm; calories from fat: 23%; cholesterol: 0 mg; sodium: 85 mg

CAESAR SALAD, Page 138
Calories: 81; carbohydrate: 6 gm; protein: 4 gm; fat: 5 gm; calories from fat: 51%; cholesterol: 39 mg; sodium: 152 mg

CARROT-CHEESE MELT, Page 124
Calories: 277; carbohydrate: 33 gm; protein: 17 gm; fat: 9 gm; calories from fat: 29%; cholesterol: 24 mg; sodium: 578 mg

CARROT SALAD, Page 126
Calories: 62; carbohydrate: 14 gm; protein: 2 gm; fat: 0 gm; calories from fat: 0%; cholesterol: 0 mg; sodium: 28 mg

CEREAL, (PERFECT BOWL OF), Page 118
Calories: 258; carbohydrate: 56 gm; protein: 11 gm; fat: 1 gm; calories from fat: 5%; cholesterol: 3 mg; sodium: 300 mg

CHEESE APPLE SURPRISE, Page 119
Calories: 197; carbohydrate: 29 gm; protein: 10 gm; fat: 5 gm; calories from fat: 23%; cholesterol: 16 mg; sodium: 294 mg

CHEESE DANISH, Page 115
USING FAT FREE CREAM CHEESE: Calories: 148; carbohydrate: 31 gm; protein: 6 gm; fat: 0 gm; calories from fat: 0%; cholesterol: 10 mg; sodium: 369 mg

USING LIGHT CREAM CHEESE: Calories: 191; carbohydrate: 31 gm; protein: 6 gm; fat: 5 gm; calories from fat: 23%; cholesterol: 10 mg; sodium: 369 mg

CHEF'S SALAD, Page 122
(without dressing) Calories: 261; carbohydrate: 29 gm; protein: 22 gm; fat: 6 gm; calories from fat: 21%; cholesterol: 42 mg; sodium: 424 mg

CHICKEN AND RICE, Page 137
Calories: 369; carbohydrate: 42 gm; protein: 27 gm; fat: 7 gm; calories from fat: 18%; cholesterol: 70 mg; sodium: 292 mg

CHICKEN, BASQUE, Page 134
WHOLE MEAL: Calories: 408; carbohydrate: 59 gm; protein: 33 gm; fat: 4 gm; calories from fat: 8%; cholesterol: 73 mg; sodium: 103 mg

CHICKEN, HAWAIIAN, Page 128
Calories: 182; carbohydrate: 5 gm; protein: 27 gm; fat: 3 gm; calories from fat: 16%; cholesterol: 72 mg; sodium: 126 mg

CHICKEN, OF THE LAND OR SEA SANDWICH, Page 123
Calories: 233; carbohydrate: 16 gm; protein: 25 gm; fat: 8 gm; calories from fat: 30%; cholesterol: 40 mg; sodium: 650 mg

CHICKEN, OVENBAKED, Page 125
Calories: 176; carbohydrate: 7 gm; protein: 27 gm; fat: 4 gm; calories from fat: 21%; cholesterol: 108 mg; sodium: 123 mg

CHICKEN, STIR-FRY, Page 135
Calories: 235; carbohydrate: 15 gm; protein: 28 gm; fat: 7 gm; calories from fat: 27%; cholesterol: 72 mg; sodium: 126 mg

CHILI, CON CARNE, Page 133
Calories: 274; carbohydrate: 24 gm; protein: 21 gm; fat: 8 gm; calories from fat: 28%; cholesterol: 47 mg; sodium: 545 mg

COLE SLAW WITH A DIFFERENCE, Page 146
    Calories: 58; carbohydrate: 13 gm; protein: 1 gm; fat: 0 gm; calories from fat: 0%;
    cholesterol: 0 mg; sodium: 20 mg

CRANBERRY SALAD MOLD, Page 148
    Calories: 84; carbohydrate: 21 gm; protein: 0 gm; fat: 0 gm; calories from fat: 0%;
    cholesterol: 0 mg; sodium: 15 mg

DATE BARS, Page 147
    Calories: 155; carbohydrate: 29 gm; protein: 4 gm; fat: 3 gm; calories from fat: 20%;
    cholesterol: 0 mg; sodium: 2 mg

DATE CHEESE BALL, Page 145
    Calories: 51; carbohydrate: 7 gm; protein: 3 gm; fat: 1 gm; calories from fat: 18%;
    cholesterol: 0 mg; sodium: 71 mg

DIP, HERB AND GARLIC, Page 146
    2 TBSP.: Calories: 20; carbohydrate: 1 gm; protein: 4 gm; fat: 0 gm; calories from
    fat: 0%; cholesterol: 1 mg; sodium: 122 mg

DIP, ZESTY, Page 145
    2 TBSP.: Calories: 16; carbohydrate: 1 gm; protein: 3 gm; fat: 0 gm; calories from
    fat: 0%; cholesterol: 1 mg; sodium: 120 mg

FRESH FRUIT PIE, Page 153
    Calories: 99; carbohydrate: 17 gm; protein: 1 gm; fat: 3 gm; calories from fat: 27%;
    cholesterol: 0 mg; sodium: 2 mg

FRENCH TOAST, Page 117
    Calories: 239; carbohydrate: 39 gm; protein: 16 gm; fat: 2 gm; calories from fat: 7%;
    cholesterol: 2 mg; sodium: 390 mg

GRAVY, HEALTHFUL, Page 149
Calories: 40; carbohydrate: 0 gm; protein: 0 gm; fat: 4.5 gm; calories from fat: all; cholesterol: 0 mg; sodium: 10 mg

GREEN BEANS AND MUSHROOMS, Page 129
Calories: 52; carbohydrate: 9 gm; protein: 2 gm; fat: 2 gm; calories from fat: 17%; cholesterol: 0 mg; sodium: 4 mg

GREEN BEANS, COLORFUL, Page 127
Calories: 53; carbohydrate: 9 gm; protein: 2 gm; fat: 1 gm; calories from fat: 17%; cholesterol: 0 mg; sodium: 4 mg

HAMBURGER, HEALTHY, Page 124
(without condiments) Calories: 261; carbohydrate: 29 gm; protein: 22 gm; fat: 6 gm; calories from fat: 21%; cholesterol: 42 mg; sodium: 424 mg

LAMB, ROSEMARY ROAST, Page 150
Calories: 254; carbohydrate: 26 gm; protein: 24 gm; fat: 7 gm; calories from fat: 23%; cholesterol: 63 mg; sodium: 281 mg

MEATLOAF, MARVELOUS, Page 127
Calories: 213; carbohydrate: 11 gm; protein: 22 gm; fat: 9 gm; calories from fat: 25%; cholesterol: 98 mg; sodium: 257 mg

MUFFINS, APPLE DATE, Page 152
Calories: 157; carbohydrate: 27 gm; protein: 4 gm; fat: 4 gm; calories from fat: 23%; cholesterol: 0 mg; sodium: 85 mg

MUFFINS, OAT BRAN, Page 120
Calories: 239; carbohydrate: 43 gm; protein: 13 gm; fat: 4 gm; calories from fat: 15%; cholesterol: 9 mg; sodium: 280 mg

OATMEAL WITH A DIFFERENCE, Page 116
  Calories: 217; carbohydrate: 38 gm; protein: 11 gm; fat: 2 gm; calories from fat: 8%; cholesterol: 3 mg; sodium: 97 mg

PARFAIT, BREAKFAST, Page 119
  Calories: 229; carbohydrate: 49 gm; protein: 10 gm; fat: 0 gm; calories from fat: 0%; cholesterol: 2 mg; sodium: 288 mg

PIZZAZ, PEACH, Page 138
  Calories: 28; carbohydrate: 7 gm; protein: less than 1 gm; fat: 0 gm; calories from fat: 0%; cholesterol: 0 mg; sodium: 5 mg

PEANUT BUTTER AND BANANA SANDWICH, Page 121
  Calories: 346; carbohydrate: 52 gm; protein: 15; fat: 9 gm; calories from fat: 23%; cholesterol: 3 mg; sodium: 378 mg

PEANUT BUTTER DANISH, Page 116
  Calories: 278; carbohydrate: 37 gm; protein: 13; fat: 9 gm; calories from fat: 30%; cholesterol: 3 mg; sodium: 278 mg

PEAS, ROSEMARY, Page 126
  Calories: 83; carbohydrate: 12 gm; protein: 4 gm; fat: 2 gm; calories from fat: 23%; cholesterol: 0 mg; sodium: 95 mg

SALMON, BAKED IN A POUCH, Page 130
  Calories: 168; carbohydrate: 3 gm; protein: 23 gm; fat: 5 gm; calories from fat: 27%; cholesterol: 42 mg; sodium: 62 mg

SALMON, GRILLED, Page 131
  Calories: 157; carbohydrate: 0 gm; protein: 23 gm; fat: 5 gm; calories from fat: 29%; cholesterol: 42 mg; sodium: 50 mg

SALMON, LOAF, Page 132
Calories: 207; carbohydrate: 13 gm; protein: 22 gm; fat: 7 gm; calories from fat: 30%; cholesterol: 72 mg; sodium: 470 mg

SALMON, POACHED, Page 131
Calories: 161; carbohydrate: 1 gm; protein: 23 gm; fat: 5 gm; calories from fat: 28%; cholesterol: 42 mg; sodium: 62 mg

SANDWICH, CLASSIC, Page 124
Calories: 241; carbohydrate: 24 gm; protein: 22 gm; fat: 6 gm; calories from fat: 24%; cholesterol: 42 mg; sodium: 424 mg

SEAFOOD, SALAD, Page 121
WHOLE MEAL: Calories: 233; carbohydrate: 16 gm; protein: 25 gm; fat: 8 gm; calories from fat: 30%; cholesterol: 40 mg; sodium: 650 mg

SHAKE, BREAKFAST, Page 118
Calories: 200; carbohydrate: 32 gm; protein: 16 gm; fat: 2 gm; calories from fat: 10%; cholesterol: 5 mg; sodium: 176 mg

SPAGHETTI PIE, Page 139
Calories: 248; carbohydrate: 21 gm; protein: 23 gm; fat: 8 gm; calories from fat: 29%; cholesterol: 46 mg; sodium: 349 mg

SPINACH AND APPLE SALAD, Page 136
Calories: 69; carbohydrate: 12 gm; protein: 1 gm; fat: 2 gm; calories from fat: 26%; cholesterol: 0 mg; sodium: 30 mg

STEAK, ITALIAN SWISS, Page 136
Calories: 345; carbohydrate: 35 gm; protein: 35 gm; fat: 6.5 gm; calories from fat: 17%; cholesterol: 71 mg; sodium: 545 mg

SWEET POTATOES GLORIOUS, Page 151
    Calories: 82; carbohydrate: 18 gm; protein: 2 gm; fat: 0 gm; calories from fat: 22%; cholesterol: 21 mg; sodium: 15 mg

VEGGIES, MARINATED, Page 139
    Calories: 67; carbohydrate: 8 gm; protein: 2 gm; fat: 3 gm; calories from fat: 40%; cholesterol: 0 mg; sodium: 340 mg

VEGGIE SANDWICH, Page 123
    Calories: 294; carbohydrate: 31 gm; protein: 20 gm; fat: 10 gm; calories from fat: 30%; cholesterol: 32 mg; sodium: 592 mg

WALDORF IN DISGUISE SALAD, Page 132
    Calories: 114; carbohydrate: 22 gm; protein: 2 gm; fat: 2 gm; calories from fat: 18%; cholesterol: 0 mg; sodium: 53 mg

WILD RICE PILAF, Page 129
    Calories: 122; carbohydrate: 21 gm; protein: 4 gm; fat: 2 gm; calories from fat: 22%; cholesterol: 0 mg; sodium: 210 mg

OTHER BOOKS AND TAPES
BY PAMELA M. SMITH, R.D.

Eat Well - Live Well
The nutrition guide and cookbook for healthy, productive people. This large, hardback edition presents "The Ten Commandments of Good Nutrition" in detail, cooking tips, menu planning, grocery shopping, a dining-out guide and a large cookbook section of innovative recipes that can be prepared in a time-saving manner. Meal plans are also included.

The Food Trap
As she explores our relationship with food, Pamela Smith asks, *Is the refrigerator light the light of your life?* Informative and enlightening, this book reveals case studies and personal insights into the physical, emotional, and spiritual aspects of food dependencies. Learn how to break free in all areas.

The Food Trap Seminar
In this audio tape album from a live seminar, Pamela Smith discusses our physical, emotional, and spiritual needs and how to meet and nourish these needs properly. She also presents a nutritional strategy for dealing with stress. Very practical and informative.

Free Tape Offer
For a free audio-cassette tape on nutrition principles by Pamela Smith, please complete and mail the following coupon (plus U.S. $2.00 to cover postage and handling).

- -

Please send me a free copy of "Nutrition Principles" Audio Tape
by Pamela Smith.
I have enclosed U.S. $2.00 to cover postage and handling.

Name:_____

Address:_____

City: _____ State: _____ Zip Code:_____

Send coupon and money to:
Pamela M. Smith, R.D. • P.O. Box 541009 • Orlando, FL 32854

Published in Nashville, Tennessee, by Thomas Nelson, Inc., Publishers, and distributed in Canada by Word Communications, Ltd., Richmond, British Columbia, and in the United Kingdom by Word (UK), Ltd., Milton Keynes, England.

Library of Congress information

Smith, Pamela M.
  Alive and well in the fast lane! / by Pamela Smith and Carolyn Coats.
      p.   cm.
  "Revised 1993."
  Originally published: Orlando, Fla. : Carolyn Coats' Bestsellers, 1987.
  Includes index.
  ISBN: 0-7852-8050-2
  1. Nutrition. I. Coats, Carolyn, 1935- . II. Title. RA784.S594 1994
613.2—dc20

93-43101
CIP

Printed in the United States of America

1 2 3 4 5 6 7 - 99 98 97 96 95 94

LOOK FOR THESE OTHER BOOKS BY CAROLYN COATS AND PAMELA SMITH

Things Your Mother Always Told You But You Didn't Want to Hear
Warm, witty, nostalgic words of wisdom you'll remember forever with love.
ISBN 0-7852-8056-1

Things Your Dad Always Told You But You Didn't Want to Hear
Funny, profound, memorable. The perfect companion to the "Mother" book. Great for men's and boys' birthday gifts.
ISBN 0-7852-8055-3

My Grandmother Always Said That
From generation to generation, grandmothers have always said the same wise words to their families. They do it because they love them, but mostly because they just can't help it.
ISBN 0-7852-8053-7

Me, A Gourmet Cook?
A delightful cookbook full of easy but delicious recipes and creative, entertaining ideas. Perfect for graduation and new brides and grooms.
ISBN 0-7852-8052-9

Alive and Well in the Fast Lane
The very latest information on how to lower your cholesterol and risk of cancer; how to increase your energy and stamina and achieve your ideal weight. The 10 Commandments of good nutrition plus great recipes and tips.
ISBN 0-7852-8050-2

Perfectly Pregnant!
The latest information to perfectly nourish you and your baby —hints to overcome morning sickness, assure ideal weight gain, and maintain your energy and stamina. The perfect gift for that "special lady."
ISBN 0-7852-8054-5

Come Cook With Me!
Shhh . . . Don't tell the kids, but this wonderful book has recipes that are delicious, fun to make AND nutritious. The gift every grandmother and parent will love to give.
ISBN 0-7852-8051-0

Available at fine bookstores everywhere.
THOMAS NELSON PUBLISHERS
Nashville, Tennessee 37214